THE DWARFS OF
MOUNT ATLAS

THE DWARFS OF MOUNT ATLAS

Collected Papers on the
Curious Anthropology of
Robert Grant Haliburton

Coachwhip Publications
Landisville, Pennsylvania

The Dwarfs of Mount Atlas
Copyright © 2009 Coachwhip Publications

ISBN 1-930585-96-9
ISBN-13 978-1-930585-96-6

Cover: Atlas Mountains © Jaroslaw Grudzinski

Coachwhipbooks.com

CONTENTS

Preface

Chad Arment

I ran across mention of Haliburton's Mount Atlas pygmy research many years ago, but only in the past few years (thanks to the expansion of online databases) was I able to discover exactly what he proposed. Robert Haliburton was an aging lawyer in the 1890s, enthused about stories he picked up in his travels in Morocco about a dwarf tribe in the inaccessible reaches of the Atlas Mountains and vicinity. Piecing together details from eyewitness stories, cobbling linguistic clues to each other, and delving into ancient legends, he argued for the existence of a tribal group of small stature distinct from its neighbors. (Given the recent discovery of Congo pygmies, this was not a far-fetched idea at the time.) But was this "hidden people" just a mirage? Contemporary critics suggested as much, just as others weighed in with their own sightings and theories. When Haliburton died, however, the stories died with him. I have seen no record of further anthropological investigations to prove or discredit the tales. True or not, they simply disappeared. Perhaps we should consider this a cautionary tale, but I have to wonder if those mountains still hold a secret.

Notes on Mount Atlas
and Its Traditions

R. G. Haliburton

In December, 1881, to while away the time at Tangier, where continuous east winds for weeks kept invalids within doors, I turned my attention to the traditions and folk-lore of the natives of Morocco. The field was represented as a barren one. I was told that the country was inhabited mainly by the Berbers (or Barbars, whence the name Barbary); that, though composed of different tribes, they spoke substantially the same language; and that, having adopted the religion of Islam, they had forgotten their old traditions and superstitions. The Riffians, known still in history as the Riff pirates, inhabit the northern portions of Mount Atlas. To the south of that mountain is a tribe of excellent artificers in brass and copper, called Shelluhs, Shilhas or Shilhachs, who inhabit the Province of Sus, and are therefore, called Susis. There are other tribes still farther south.

It soon leaked out that the faith of Islam sits very lightly on some of the Susis, and that many of them really have no religion, or have some ancient superstitions which they preserve in secret. Whether they really believe the myths and traditions which they repeated to me, or merely regard them as our peasants do their fairy tales and folk-lore, it is hard to decide. One of them told me he was not sure that he was not as much of a Christian as of a Mohammedan—a statement that, if overhead by the Moors, might have cost him his life.

I made careful enquiries from several Riffians, a Maltese who had travelled in the interior of Africa, disguised as a Moor, the town time-keeper or astronomer at Tangier, some Jews of Casablanca and Ophran, two Susis at Tangier and one at Mogador, nearly all of whom, though illiterate, and unable to read Arabic, were learned in oral tradition and Berber folk-lore.

The results of my enquiries proved that there is a marvellous collection of ancient myths, legends, etc., among the Susis, which carry us in succession to Britain, Greece and Rome, Phoenicia and Egypt, and even to Babylon, while one very remarkable festival seems as if it had reached them from the Aztecs, or vice versa.

The Great Mother of the Greeks, Damater, appeared as *Ta Mata*, "the mother, who presides over the corn fields." Apalo, "a good god, who comes and plays on a harp," suggests the enquiry, is not Apalo the original form of the name of the god Apollo? [1]

At certain intervals, as the Greeks believed, Apollo used to desert his shrines, and go far off to the blessed Hyperboreans of Mount Atlas, with whom he danced and sang until the rising of the Pleiades.

The ancient Greeks themselves seem to have regarded the Atlas country as the favorite abode of Apollo. Atlas was a Hyperborean, and the western Ethiopians who inhabited that country were also Hyperboreans, a semi-divine race, from whom the Greeks derived many of their most ancient rites. It is supposed that they were called Hyperboreans from their enjoying a climate where the cold north wind was unknown,[2] but the same name would be even more applicable to the people of the interior of Africa.

A Susi described to me a staff ornamented with ribbons, which is called a *thurosis!* The names, too, of Mata, Kera and Zerea recall that of Ceres. The "Great Mother's" image is bathed at the end of her festival, as it was in the holy island of the Germans, at the River Almon, and in Athens at a feast of Minerva, which was, therefore, called *Plynteria*. We are even reminded of a similar rite at the end of the feast of the god of agriculture of the Fijians.

The god Adon is still believed to have been slain by a boar, and heaven and earth all weep for him. "He was greatly beloved by Tachal and Isai." It seems that some festive dirges, like the Maneros of the Egyptians and the Linus of the Greeks, which were sung at their banquets, can still be traced in the *Accasili Maneros* and the *Walinas* of the Susis. Diodorus Siculus tells us that in the Atlas country a divine youth, Hesperus, went up at night to the summit of a mountain to study the stars, and a great wind carried him away. To this day (I am told by the Susis) "the women go up on the mountains with music, weeping, in their search for Walinas. He was the brother of Panis, an old god who invented pipes called Kraf or Kalifer, and who was also called Itada."

One of the Susis asked me if I would like to hear "the story of the man who wished to steal the cows," and, upon being asked to proceed, retailed a familiar bit of classical mythology: "There is a great mountain in the sea, where there were three hundred cows, the property of Geryon,[3] and when the sun set they used to appear. It was a very rich place, and a navigator, who wished to steal the cows, sailed thither and entered a great cave, from which he never came out; and his name was Herakles."

There can be no question that this mountain, the true Mount Atlas, was the Peak of Teneriffe, in which there is a vast cave that has never been fully explored. The Atlas country was the scene of the labors of Hercules and of the feats of Perseus, who turned Atlas into a mountain by showing him the Gorgon's head.

Herodotus says that the dress of the statue of Minerva was borrowed from the Atlas country, where clothes of kidskin were made and colored with great skill. Such dresses may still be seen in the Museum of Las Palmas, taken from the mummy caves of the Guanches. He also suggests that the story of the head of Medusa being encircled with snakes, arose from the head having been placed on a shield ornamented by the Atlantes with a fringe consisting of long strips of leather, which at a distance might well look like snakes. These fringes are still used by the Susis.

Even the Greeks admitted that one of their most unintelligible myths, that of the fifty daughters of Danaus, who were doomed in hell to the task of filling sieves with water, came from Africa, and they, therefore, gave the brother of the Danaides the name of Egyptus, though modern Egyptologists have failed to meet with the myth in the religion of the ancient Egyptians. Many years ago a devout believer in "Arkite lore" detected an allusion to the deluge in the name of Danaus, which he traced to *dan*, "water" or "rain." If he had called the fable a "rain myth," he would perhaps have been nearer the mark. It was evidently carried by the natives of the Atlas to Greece, where in time its original meaning was forgotten, for we still find it in the folk-lore of the Susis, one of whom told me that "there is an old king in the stars of rain, who has many dancing women, who hold sieves filled with water; and when he wishes them to dance, he thunders. The louder grow the peals, the quicker grows the dance, during which the sieves are emptied, and the water falls to the earth in a thunder shower." [4]

These are a few only of the traditions and beliefs that carry us to Greece and Rome. We meet with Phoenician traditions also as to "Isiri, who taught the three letters"; while the belief in an imperfect creation, in which the forms of animals and men were blended together, recalls a similar tradition of the old Chaldeans.[5] Of Egyptian ideas there are perhaps traces in a belief as to seven brothers who sail in their ship across the sky, and carry with them the spirits of the dead.

The Susis have a May Day festival, at which the "pole of Maia " is set up, at the summit of which is a doll composed of heads of wheat. Saints climb up the tree and scatter the wheat among the people, calling it "our life," "our sustenance." The Mexicans used to erect an enormous cross, the symbol of rain, and on its summit was placed a similar doll, which, when reached by those climbing the pole, was scattered among the people, who treasured the fragments as something sacred, while the deity represented was called "our life," "our support." The coincidence is certainly very remarkable, for precisely the same words were addressed by the Iroquois to the three beneficent maidens who brought each her gift to mortals, the maize, the squash and the bean.

Herodotus has mentioned that the peculiar cry of the women at the rites of Minerva, called *ololuzein*, was borrowed from the Libyan women, "who sing it very sweetly." I have heard this peculiar chorus or cry, which consists of a quick repetition of the word alo—alo alo alo alo. I am told that it is raised at the end of the feast of Mata, when water is poured over the image of the goddess; and am reminded of the shout that resounded throughout Fiji at the close of the feast of Ratimaimbulu, who no doubt was the same as the god Alo-alo of the adjacent Friendly or Tonga Islands. It would be exceedingly interesting if it should prove that the cry raised and carried from town to town in Fiji was, like that at the feast of Mata, *alo alo alo alo.*

If there is any foundation for the belief of the earliest nations, and of the Susis themselves, that that country was once the seat of an ancient civilization, how can we account for the early rise of a great commercial and maritime people near Mount Atlas? The answer may be given in one word—gold. One of the natives examined at Mogador was Mordecai Rhibo, a Jew from Ophran, which he described as a very ancient town, which from remote ages has been the *entrepôt* of the Timbuctoo gold trade. At that point the caravans separate, and go in different directions, one to the city of Morocco, and the other beyond Tripoli.

There are very ancient Jewish tombstones there. There is also a vague tradition there that there is somewhere in

the interior a tribe of Jews who are warlike and independent, and who have no knowledge of the Second Temple,

I ventured to suggest, when I read my paper, that we
have good reason to believe that the *Ophir* of the Bible and
Saba or *Sheba* may yet be traced to that part of Africa. This
has since been confirmed by my finding in Procopius that
one of the two great divisions of Mauritania was called
Zaba. He also states that there was in his day (circ. A.D.
550) a very ancient city in Numidia, on the borders of
Mauritania, called *Borium*, which from the most remote
times had been inhabited by Jews, who had never paid tribute to any one. There was there, too, a very remarkable
Jewish temple, which the Jews believed had been built by
King Solomon. As the adjoining country was called Zaba,
and as no trace of the first temple has ever been found in
Jerusalem, it is not impossible that this was the temple to
which the Queen of Sheba paid her famous visit.

It is probable that nomad Berbers, known as Sabaeans,
had, in the days of Abraham, as they still have, the mono-
poly of the gold and ivory trade of central Africa, and with
their caravans carried its products, including slaves, par-
rots and incense, to central Asia.[6] The Sabaeans were, like
the Susis, astrologers, necromancers, traders and robbers,
believing in the seven heavens, and worshipping the seven
stars. It has been conjectured that in the Puranas traditions
of an earthly paradise differing from that of the general
Hindoo system seem to point to Africa (see Smith's Dictionary of Bible, tit. "Eden"). But the place to which we
must turn cannot be, as Smith's article suggests, in southern Africa, but rather in north-western Africa, where the

garden of the Hesperides and the Islands of the Blessed were situated.

The Susis have a belief in seven heavens called *Saba Samagwats*. Saba means seven; the other word, by the aid of a pre-Malayan language in Malacca, can be interpreted, as it is the same as samangats, "the spirits of the blessed," who reside in Pulo Bua, "the fruitful island in the west." I have also been shown a diagram of the mystic ladder for the descent and ascent of souls, called *Azacol*, representing "the path of the spirits" (*Azero*). It is like the ladder with seven lamps that typified the seven "houses" or "gates of heaven" in the rites of Mithra. These Susis are necromancers and astrologers, resembling the gypsies in looks, habits and ideas. One of them at the outset offered to bring up any spirit that I might wish to do my bidding, an offer that recalled the question of the Witch of Endor, "And the woman said, whom shall I bring up unto thee?"

To show how indestructible the peculiar traditions of these people are, I may mention that a Susi told me gravely of a remarkable race at the River Byblah (Byblus?), "which is near the centre of the world, somewhere between us and the Soudan," who have the faces of dogs. Herodotus, 2,500 years ago, was told precisely the same story, a belief in which among the Egyptians can be traced in their mystic *cynocephali*.[7]

It may seem premature to endeavor to account for this strange collection of myths from apparently all parts of the world. A few facts connected with the history of Mount Atlas may be suggestive of interesting enquiries.

The earliest traditions of Greece point to Mount Atlas and to the garden of the Hesperides, which was on the flank of that mountain. The Susis told me that their people is the most ancient in the world. Diodorus Siculus says that the Atlantes claimed to be the most ancient of nations, and that their country was "the birthplace of all the gods of antiquity." Solon was told by the Egyptian priests the same tale, that the Atlantes were the first great commercial and maritime people, and exceeded in wealth all the great nations of later times, and that they extended their conquests as far as Greece; but in consequence of a sudden irruption of the sea, the great island they inhabited was buried under the waves in a single night. History proves, too, that the Berber race was once dominant over northern Africa, and it is probable that they supplied the Hycsos, or Shepherd dynasty, that ruled over Egypt for centuries, and who have been connected with the Moors and Berbers by Movers.

One of the names of the Atlantes was *Maxyans*, which is possibly derived from a word in Arabic meaning "sheep." Atlas, who, as a daring navigator, "knew all the depths of the ocean," and who taught Hercules astronomy, was also called "a shepherd." The Susis (at least the nomad portion of them) are still called by the Arabs *Beni Baccar*, "the sons of the cow," the pastoral people. Even the word "Sos," according to Herodotus, meant in the sacred language of Egypt "cattle."

It has been conjectured that the light-haired race, that from the most remote ages occupied the Atlas country, lost their language and adopted the Berber tongue.

That Tarshish was a port in the Atlas country seems exceedingly probable. It is admitted that it was situated either in Spain or somewhere on the Atlantic seaboard. It was apparently the Birmingham of early ages, for its brazen dishes were an extensive article of export even to Phoenicia. We have now no trace of such an industry in Spain, but we have the clearest evidence that from the most remote times it flourished in Sus, the people of which seem to be a survival from the Bronze Age, for their principal trade is the manufacture of brass dishes, which they chase with marvellous taste, and which are perhaps known to us as the "beaten dishes" used in the Temple of Solomon. Leo Africanus says that Ifran was in his time (A. D., 1550) a seat of this industry, from the existence of extensive copper mines near that place. Though it is only known throughout Morocco as *Ephran*, its inhabitants call it Ophran, and such is the name given to it in the latest English map of that country.[8]

To the ancient Jews it was probably known as Ophir, that mysterious city which tradition says was the capital of the Sabaeans, and connected with Tarshish. That the latter was a port of Ophir or Ophran, and situated on the coast of Sus,[9] seems probable from some curious incidents in the history of Jonah, who instead of going eastward from Jerusalem to Nineveh, went to the remotest west, in a ship bound to Tarshish.

To my surprise one day, a Susi told me that a great prophet was swallowed by a large fish and cast up by it on the coast of Sus, and I at first assumed that he had picked up this story from some Jew; but I have since discovered that it is an ancient local tradition as to Hercules, the hero of the Atlas, who must have sailed from a port in western Morocco, for on ancient maps we find a harbor there called "the port of Hercules." The two stories (whichever may have been the original one) point to a tradition connected with the Atlantic and the coast of Sus.

Many myths have a local origin in some natural phenom-
enon that primitive races cannot explain, except by the super-
natural. We may find the key to this venerable tradition of
antiquity as to Hercules in the existence, near the place in
question, of sharp pointed rocks, which are fatal to whales
that may be driven on them by a storm. Hercules, we are
told (see Took's Pantheon, Part II, ch. I; Ovid Met., II)
"delivered Hesione, the daughter of Laomedon, King of Troy,
from the whale in this manner; he raised, on a sudden, a
bank in the place where Hesione was to be devoured, and
stood armed before it; and when the whale came seeking
his prey, Hercules leaped into his mouth, slided down his
throat, destroyed him, and came away safe."

The tradition, which I had heard from a Susi, also existed
in the days of Leo Africanus, who tells us that in the town
of Messa, the name of which means "Lord," and at which
the natives believe that the promised Messiah will appear,
is a very ancient and sacred temple, the rafters of which all
consist of the bones of whales, in commemoration of a
prophet having been cast up by a whale on the adjacent
seashore; and that in confirmation of this belief, the Moors
pointed to the fact that all the whales immediately die that
pass to the right of the temple. The historian was inclined
to think that there might be something in the story, from
his seeing at the time a dead whale floating near; but a Jew
ridiculed the superstition of the Moors, and explained the
origin of it—by the existence and effects of the reef in question—that bank, no doubt, that Hercules raised suddenly
for the destruction of the whale. I think there can be little
question that this ancient whalebone temple of Jonah was

originally built in honor of Hercules, the hero of the Atlas country; and it is possible that the story connected with it may have been carried back to Palestine by the Jews of Ophir, and have been preserved by them in the history of the prophet Jonah.

May not they also have brought back from Ophir the Book of Job? That work is a singularly faithful picture of the productions, animals, traditions, manners and astronomical ideas that are still to be found south of Mount Atlas.[10] There to this day wandering bands from the desert sweep down upon the herdsman and the shepherd, and rob them of their herds and flocks; and the ostrich, the hippopotamus, the monsters of the ocean, the birds, the beasts, the treasures of the mine, and the stars that are described by the patriarch, are still familiar to its inhabitants. Even that auspicious constellation whose "sweet influences" are celebrated by him, is known by the same name to the Susis, who call it *Kimah* ("a furrow" or "cornhill"), or "the stars of tillage" as it is termed by the far distant Bechuanas of South Africa (*Silemela*).

The people of Sus also believe that there is a certain night in the year when the stars hold a solemn festival, in which all the angels and the spirits of the great kings of old take part. The very words of the song of the Pleiades, who are known in the New World as well as in the Old as "the dancers," "the Celestial chorus" of the Greeks, "the Heavenly Host" of the Hebrews, and "the seven dancers " of the North American Indians, are familiar to ears that can catch "the music of the spheres," and have been repeated to me by one of those favored mortals, a Susi wanderer from the Sahara:

"Oh Moon, oh Mother, we hold our feast to-night.
   We are dancing before God, between heaven and earth,"

words that recall Milton's allusion to those "morning stars that sang together with joy" at the creation,

"And the Pleiades before him danced.
   Shedding sweet influences."

also

"The gray dawn and the Pleiades,
   Shedding 'sweet influences'."

This celestial festival evidently takes place on that night in November, when the full moon and the Pleiades are on the meridian together, for there is a Susi love song,

"Oh come to me my love, and long remain,
   For the Pleiades are meeting the moon to-night."

On that very night in November some tribes of the Australians still celebrate "the sweet influences of the Pleiades," and hold a grand corroboree in their honor, for "they are the children of the Sun and Moon," and "are very good to the black-fellows."

Even the early Egyptians seem to have borrowed many of their religious ideas from an older civilization in the Atlas country, for it has been conjectured that all the magical features of the ritual of the Egyptians, and their belief as to the dangers attending the passage of the soul to Hades, were derived from the people south of the Atlas (see Smith's Dict. of the Bible, tit., "magic").

It is surprising to find that a country, venerated in the days of Homer as peopled by "the just Ethiopians" who were nearer to the gods than other men, and at whose banquets even Jupiter was sometimes a guest, a country, too, associated with paradise and the abodes of the blessed, should, a few hundred years after his time, have been lost sight of by the world.[11] Herodotus does not refer to its past history, and learned little of the country south of the Atlas. Strabo says that in his time it was a *terra incognita*, for armies and even travellers had seldom reached it, and the few natives that visited Greece either invented fables about it, or were unwilling to tell what they knew about it. To this day it is closed against Europeans, none being able to visit it except by the hazardous experiment of passing for a Moor.

Leo Africanus, however, himself a Moor, who has described that country as it appeared in his day, and has told us how the Arabs had ravaged it, destroying the cities, and burning the ancient books of the Berbers, states that near the walls of one town, the stones of which, as large as those employed in the construction of the Coliseum at Rome, had defied the fury of the invaders, gold and silver medals are to be found, with characters which he had in vain endeavored to decipher; and that everything indicates that at a former period these cities must have been the homes of a prosperous people.

This paper is the first attempt that has been made to draw attention to the traditions of a country that must once have played an important role in history. It is possible that future and more careful enquiries as to it may throw much light on the commerce, and perhaps on the origin of the Jews, and on many obscure points connected with early civilizations and mythologies; and that they may even prove that the belief of the Susis and of the old Atlantes, that their land was "the birth-place of all the gods of antiquity" was not a baseless one.

I intend, if my health permits me, to revisit that country, and to follow up these researches.

FOOTNOTES

[1] Aplo is the Etruscan name for Apollo.

[2] The ancients believed in three zones, the highest of which was above the winter winds, and was the abode of the gods. Olympus was such a paradise.

[3] There is a tribe in the Atlas called Alt Gerouan.

[4] Grimm says that the Pleiades (those stars of rain) were called in European mythology "The Sieves." This myth may explain why throughout Africa, when it thunders, It is said "heaven beats," *i.e.*, beats time to the dancers.

[5] According to one of my Susi informants, the Alissawa rites symbolize this idea by men representing wild beasts, while the fat Moor on horseback represents the Good Spirit who civilized primeval man. This was the origin of *mumming* among the ancients and modern savages.

[6] There is a priestly tribe near the northern limits of the Sahara, called *Oulad-bu-Saba*, or *Sabaeen*, who guide caravans to Timbuctoo, steering by the Pleiades, not by the Pole Star. When a Susi is in

great peril, he ejaculates "Oulad-bu-Saba," just as an Italian peasant in a like case invokes the saints.

[7] Mr. Walter B. Harris (see "Dwarfs of Mount Atlas," p. 3) says: "I
have often been asked by Moors whether it was true that there
was a race of people in the south known as Beni Kerbou, with dogs'
heads; and also a race with one eye (Cyclops). Beni Kerbou means
'the sons of dogs'" (see "Dwarfs of Mount Atlas," pp. 28, 29,
30). At Pount, in southern Morocco, there are little images with
heads of dogs, called "Makerbu." There was a people there called
by the Greeks "Macrobu" (the long-lived), for the Greeks, like
many of our college professors, derived everything from Greek.

[8] The far-famed "brazen gates of the wall of Agloo" were made at
Ophran, sometimes called *Ophiran*.

[9] *Sus*, a country bounding on the Atlantic, and south of the Atlas, is
called *Ta-Sus* ("the Sus"). The River Sus is called *Assif na Ta-
Sus* ("the river of the Sus ").

[10] Job is held in great reverence in southern Morocco, and is the patron saint of more than one tribe. We meet with one called *Beni
Joub* ("the sons of Job").

[11] Ionian and Carian mercenaries were largely employed not only by
the Pharaohs, but also by the Libyans, thousands of years before the
time of Homer, who must have been familiar with the history, the
traditions, and the position of the Atlas country. The Ionians divided
the world into four quarters, one of which was not Egypt, but Libya.
In time these mercenaries ceased to be employed in North Africa,
and as the Carthaginians kept all strangers out of that country,
the later Greeks lost almost all knowledge of the geographical
position of Mount Atlas, and even transferred it and its myths to
the Danube, and to the Caucasus. Hence we have the Amazons of
Libya and of Asia, and an African and an Asiatic Hercules, etc.

THE DWARFS OF MOUNT ATLAS

Statements of Natives of Morocco and of European Residents There as to the Existence of a Dwarf Race South of the Great Atlas

R. G. Haliburton

PREFACE

If it is conclusively settled, as it will be, I hope, ere long, that there is a race of dwarfs South of Mount Atlas, I fear I shall not be able to claim much credit for my having made the discovery, for it required very little sagacity to understand, when told by my servant, a highly intelligent Susi, that in Akka, within a hundred miles or so of his native place, there was a race of dwarfs only four feet high, that the story, if true, was very important in an ethnological point of view, and should be looked into. It will be seen that there is really no shadow of excuse for gross personalities in this discussion, as will be clear on reading the evidence which I have been tempted to publish on the subject. It must be remembered that the two men who stand far above all others as authorities on Morocco and the Moors, and who have each spent a lifetime in that country, agree with me in my views. A part of Mr. Hunot's letter is published among the evidence. As for the Right Hon. Sir J. Drummond-Hay, all the world has known of him and his family in connection with Morocco for three-quarters of a century. His father was Minister there before him, and he himself ably represented our country there for over forty years, and almost a half century ago wrote the only work we have which throws any light on the folk-lore and festivals of Western Barbary.

Purves Hall, Greenlaw, N. B.
30th September, 1891.

Dear Mr. Haliburton,

During my long residence in Morocco, upwards of half-a-century, I ought, as may be expected, to be well acquainted with that country and its inhabitants. Though I have travelled frequently in the interior where the Moors and Arabs reside, I have never ventured to penetrate into the mountainous districts, inhabited by wild Berber races, except on the Northern slopes of the Atlas. The Berbers of the South differ from the Northern people, as much as Gipsies do from the English peasantry.

They are an intelligent race, skilled as smiths, tinkers, well-sinkers, makers of leather, acrobats, jugglers, fortune-tellers, and professional seekers for buried treasure, and are in possession, as it has come to my knowledge sometimes, of documents and oral traditions about treasure hidden by their forefathers. You were the first to make the Berbers dwelling on the Southern slopes of the Atlas a special subject of study, when you commenced researches ten years ago, and since then you have, in a great measure, been alone in enquiries regarding their legends and beliefs, and have devoted, to my knowledge, much time in patient research, and have taken infinite pains, at some considerable expense, to obtain information as to this unknown field. With regard to the present controversy raised regarding the existence of a dwarf race, I remember in 1888 you wrote to me, from Algeria, about your servant, a native of Soos, having stated that there was in Akka, the country adjoining the Soos district he came from, a race of dwarfs about four feet high, having a reddish complexion, differing from that of the Moors, Arabs, Berbers, or negroes. On enquiries made by me regarding these dwarfs, I found a man from Dra, who described a similar race of dwarfs dwelling at or near Akka, a district adjoining Soos. It is also, as you are aware, a fact that there is a district called Akka near the Albert Nyanza, with a precisely similar race of dwarfs, a coincidence which we can hardly suppose to be a chance one. I had also a late opportunity of questioning a native of Dra on the subject of dwarfs, and he gave without hesitation, and as I am led to believe truthfully, the same account as my previous informant, whom he did not know I had examined; but he said that the Dra dwarfs are called the Little

Harateen. He described them as being about four feet high with a red complexion, and short woolly hair. He said 'they are very active, and are more ancient than the larger Harateen, who are sprung from them and resemble them in colour and ways, but are taller from intermarrying with other races. The small people are called "Baraka" or Oulad Mebrok, the Blessed Tribe, or Sons of the Blessed, and are supposed to bring good luck, so we do not like to talk about them.'

It does not appear that the dwarfs are as numerous in North as in Equatorial Africa, but *of their existence I have little doubt. I have met individuals occasionally of this race*, as described, before I knew of the interest which is at present attached to these people, and so had not taken an opportunity of conversing with them.

I regret to have seen articles and letters addressed to public journals calling in question the accuracy of the interesting account you gave at the Oriental Congress of the Dwarf Race in Morocco. I hope you will ere long publish for the benefit of the literary world the result of your researches regarding the history of the people dwelling on the Southern slopes of the Atlas.

I remain,

Yours very truly,

J. H. Drummond Hay

I have received a letter from Mr. W. B. Harris, which shows that pro or con, the subject of the dwarfs is likely to be cleared up before a year elapses. In it he says, "I am intensely interested in the dwarf question, and intend leaving for Morocco in November, when I shall make every possible inquiry about the subject, and I hope to meet with success. *Of the existence of dwarf tribes there I have absolutely no doubt.* While in the interior, I made the acquaintance of a leading Moor, who told me that such dwarf tribes existed, and that he was yearly visited by three or four dwarfs on business. I have often been asked by Moors whether it was true that there was a race of people to the South known as Beni Kerbou, with dog's heads, and also a race with one eye. Beni Kerbou means, 'the sons of dogs.'"

It turns out that not much more than a hundred miles from the French frontier, in the country inhabited by the Beni Znassen, and in the Ait Atta country, near the head waters of the river Did, there are towns or villages of these dwarfs, which could probably be reached by competent explorers, if reticent as to the object of their travels.

Thirty-five natives, who are from every important district from the Atlantic to Tafilelt, state that towns or hamlets of these dwarfs are to be found at or near the following places, viz.:—in Akka, at or near Akairi, Akka-Igan, Guil, Itonayli, Tamzrat, and Tadakoust, and also in the mountains of Kaleez; at Tazzawalt in Sas; and also a few in Haha, and Schedma; in the Dra Valley, at or near Taurirt, Ait Tinker, Ait Souk, Ait Sheltar, Tamanart, and Valley of Imini; south-east of Dra, at or near Asa, Atoum-ribet, Tasker-Yekn-ishet, Bani-Youssi, and River Dora of Didoo, near Tinzone; East of Demnat, at or near Ait Messad, Ait Messal, and Ait Bensid, in the Ait Atta country; in the country of the Beni Znassen; and at Iguilmim, in the Sahel.

"There is safety in numbers" in this matter, as to not only my sixty-five informants, but also my interpreters, ten of whom, in all, were successively employed by me between November and June last, and all of whom spoke Arabic either as their native language, or as fluently as natives. No European can speak Shilhach, the language of Southern Morocco, but most of the natives of that country, that come to Northern cities, speak Arabic, and two or three of my Shilhach informants were able to speak English.

The following is an extract from a letter recently addressed to Mr. Meakin by myself:—

"The country South of Mount Atlas is a perfectly distinct one from that north of that range. Mr. Hunot of Saffi, the best authority on Morocco as to the Moors, though living so far South, admitted to me that he knew little or nothing of Southern Morocco. You do not profess to lecture on the Sus and Dra country. You have never been there nor made it a special subject of inquiry, and De Foucauld's few fragmentary bits of information as to the people there, are all that can be gleaned from books. You are aware that I am the only living man that has made their beliefs and traditions a special study, and that it is ten years since I began my investigations. I had been at work some years before De Foucauld found his way there, and before you reached the happy land of Morocco. I have been surprised to find how thin is the Moslem veneer on these people, and how deep-seated are their superstitions and old beliefs."

It is very desirable that European residents at Fez, the city of Morocco, Mogador, and Saffi, should enquire from *new arrivals* from Southern Morocco as to these dwarfs, for many of the Moors in the towns cannot be depended on in such matters; and that attention should be specially drawn to the localities I have named, as this will render both the questions and the answers more definite.

The italics used in printing the statements of natives, &c., are in most cases intended to draw attention to the evidence as to there being tribes of dwarfs, and not merely a few families.

Thirty-five native informants have testified on that point, and the most important of their statements respecting it are now published. The total number of natives, European residents, and travellers who have seen one or more of these dwarfs, or have testified as to the existence of a dwarf race, amounts to sixty-five.

As superstitious Moors may resent the truth being told to Christians as to these dwarfs, I have omitted the names of my native informants.

P.S.—After the MSS. was placed in the printer's hands, a Moor, who speaks English fluently, made a statement in presence of H. W. Bates, Esq., Assistant Secretary of the Royal Geographical Society, which will be found at the end of the evidence.

The Dwarfs of Mount Atlas

The paper read on this subject at the Oriental Congress on Sept. 2nd, has attracted so much attention, and created so much discussion, that it is desirable to have the statements of natives and others on the subject placed within the reach of those who are interested in such questions, especially as one editorial has summed up the proof of the existence of a dwarf race South of Mount Atlas, as consisting of the statements of "two or three stray Englishmen," while another paper has asserted that only "two or three natives could be found" who would admit that they had any knowledge of such a race. The best way to comment on such reckless criticism is to publish the evidence.

But before going into the testimony in support of the existence of this race of dwarfs I may refer to an unwillingness on the part of many natives to speak of them, arising probably from the belief that it is not lucky to do so, which prevents an Irish peasant from mentioning the name of the "fairies," who are only called "the little people," "the good people," "the gentry," &c., a vestige of the influence in the earliest ages of a worship of a dwarf race.

In 1881, I commenced investigations into the beliefs, traditions, and ethnology of the races that inhabit the country South of the Great Atlas, many of whom come to Northern towns in caravans, or as acrobats, or wandering fortune-tellers, or cunning workers in silver, brass, and leather. Up to that date, and for several years afterwards, I was the only person who had made these people a subject of study. The Moors, North of the Atlas, seemed to know as little as Europeans do of that Southern land. While jotting down some

of the legends which I was told by a few of the people of
Sus or Dra whom I examined in 1882 (for many of them
would tell me nothing, or were timid or stupid), mention
was made of the "little people" by a Susi that I met at
Tangier, and also by a Taleb that was examined at Mogador.
According to the first, *"Ayusa* or *Idyl* is the name of *the
small people* that bring down Isiri and take him back." The
second said, "on that day the Adusal (*a small people*) will
appear." I never suspected that these expressions referred
to a dwarf race but assumed that they alluded to cherubs or
fairies.

The next time that I heard of these "Little People" was
while in Algeria, early in 1888.

A remarkably intelligent Susi, who had lived as a valet
or cook in England for some years, was engaged as a servant. He spoke English as fluently as an Englishman, and
had become a Christian, and nothing delighted him more
than to talk about his country and its people. His native
place was 100 miles east of Massa, *i.e.*, about two days
from Akka.[1]

One day he volunteered an account of the feast of
Ashura, where the people that attend the fairs are person-
ated with great skill. Among the persons represented he
named Akkas, and Jews, and was proceeding to describe
the peculiar dress and look of the Sus Jews, when I asked
him "who are these Akkas?" He then described them as a race
of little people, not higher than four feet, and of a peculiar
reddish colour, "like that of a Red Indian of America," and
differing from the complexions of Moors, Arabs, negroes,
&c. According to him they were very brave and active, and

dressed more like the French than the Moors, as they wore a woollen shirt embroidered at the neck in front and on the back. They had red leather boots or leggings coming up nearly to the knee, and their knife or dagger had a peculiar crescent-shaped handle. They made spindles and other small articles, which they sold at the markets. Their name was derived from their living in Akka, the country adjoining his own.

The story seemed so utterly incredible that I did not believe it, for I felt convinced that if there was a dwarf race so near the Mediterranean, the world would long ago have heard of them. He himself did not seem to think they would interest me, and merely mentioned them casually; and had I not brought him back to the Akkas by my wish to know who they were, he would have passed on to other subjects, and I would never have suspected that he had alluded to a dwarf race. On one point I knew he was correct, viz., that there is a district, a very barren one, between Dra and the Sahara called Akka.

The conversation was forgotten, and probably never would have been recalled to my mind but for my seeing in the *Times* and other English papers, about two months afterwards, that Emin Pasha had sent to the Royal Society skeletons of two Akkas, a dwarf race living at Akka, in the Monbutto country, who are the smallest people in the world, as they are not much over four feet in height. The complexion of these Akkas was described as "like the colour of slightly roasted coffee."

Hamed was sent for, and was asked to repeat his description of the small people about whom he had spoken to me. His account in no way varied from that which he had previously given. He could not read, and therefore could not have heard of the Albert Nyanza and its district of Akka with its dwarfs, for up to that time but little had been said about these Akkas in England, except through the works of one or two travellers. I had, unfortunately, when I was reading "The Heart of Africa," and had reached the amusing picture of a Bongo native in the second volume, been interrupted by somebody, and had never read the rest of the book. The subsequent discussion about the dwarf skeletons, and the description of Stanley's dwarfs, have made everyone familiar with the name of the Akka dwarfs near the Albert Nyanza.

I immediately wrote what had occurred to several persons in different towns in Morocco and Algeria, and asked them to hunt up some natives of Akka or Dra, or a Jew from Ophran, and to find out whether they had ever heard of a very small race of dwarfs in that country.

The first to reply to the letter was the Right Hon. Sir J. Drummond Hay, who was spending the winter there, and who had for many years been connected with Morocco as our Minister to that country. His first letter, dated May 10th, was as follows:—

"The information you had received regarding the race of men dwelling at Akka, a barren district adjoining the Dra country, is quite correct. They are described to me as a race about four feet high, broad and muscular. They are called Nezeegan. The Moor who gave my informant this account of these people, said they live on milk and camel's flesh. They pound the flesh and salt it. The pounded meat is put in goat skins, and a handful of this stuff will suffice as the sustenance of a man for two days. They are renowned for strength and courage.

"The Dra Moor said that a European, dressed as a Mahommedan, and calling himself a Shereef, visited Akka, and found there a slab with an inscription on it, and carried it off. The Akka inhabitants did not discover, until after he left, that he was not a Shereef, but a Christian disguised as a Mahommedan. I have no notion who this traveller may have been."

The second letter is dated June 6th, 1888:—

"With reference to the queries put in your letter of the 26th ultimo, the only further information I can obtain is that *the small race of men* are of a mahogany colour, with hair like that of negroes, that they use the Shilhach language, but there is a slight difference in the dialect from that spoken by the population of Sus. Berber and Shilhach are as alike as the Portuguese and Spanish languages. My informant now tells me that the tribe to which the Akka people belong is called *Ait Wakka*, and that they live in a district adjoining the Dra country.

"My informant says that the Akkas have all a similar cast of countenance, and that a stranger can hardly distinguish one adult male from another."

Again, on the 23rd June, 1888, he wrote: "My informant says that the *dwarf, or small race*, were not negroes, but dark, with features so alike that it is hard to know one from the other. Hair crisp and curly."

Miss Lena Day, belonging to the Mission to the Berbers at Tlemçen, in reply to my queries, wrote: "In reply to your letter, I have done my best to obtain information to answer your questions, but as the time you have given me is rather short, I have only been able to find one man from Sus, but he told me that the Akkas are not dwarfs, but on the average 5 feet high; but the word you mention, Nezeegan, is the name of *a tribe of dwarfs* living in a town called Nezeeg, thence their name; that the town Nezeeg is very near Sus, whereas the tribe of Ait Atta (not Atla) is some distance from Sus, though its people do frequent Sus for commerce. The Nezeegan resemble the Arabs in every particular, but their height is less than 4 feet. Their bournous is made of three and a-half yards of material. According to this man's account the Ait Atta resemble the French nation in appearance and dress, and it is said that they were once Christians, but are now Mahommedans, governed by a Cadi, and under the power of the Sultan."

Again on the 29th June, 1888, she wrote: "I have delayed answering your letter, hoping to get more reliable information, but I have only succeeded in seeing one man from Sus who has been at Nezeeg. Both men are agreed that the dwarfs are not Nigritoes."

This information obtained by separate enquiries at Tangier and Tlemçen strongly confirmed the story told me by my Susi servant. It was clear that the dwarf natives of Akka, near the Victoria Nyanza, must belong to the same race as the little natives of Akka in the Southern Atlas, as they were precisely alike in every particular, except that the one race is savage and the other is civilized. As they are both red-complexioned, it is possible that their name may be derived from *akka* (red).

It was evident that the subject ought not to be neglected, but that somebody ought to look into it in Morocco. From the state of my health I did not feel disposed to engage in an investigation which would need many months of steady work. Therefore, while passing through Paris, I called on a well-known Egyptologist, and urged him to take up the archaeology and ethnology of the Southern Atlas, and promised that I would meet him at Mogador, and would bring the natives to him who could tell him the legends and folk-lore of that region.

He was told that the God Didoo (called by Brugsch Bey a "Nubi-Libyan divinity"), one of the oldest of Egyptian gods, must have come from the country South of Mount Atlas, for rivers and tribes bear his name, viz.:—the district of Did or Didan; the Ait Didi, or Didoo, Ait Hedidoo, and Ait Doodoon; the river *Did* (which by its junction with the Idermi forms the Dra), and the river Didoo or Dora, in the Black Mountains, near Tinzone, a range of the Bani Mountains; while the name of the god *Didoo Osiris* is known South of the Atlas as *Didoo Isiri*. It has since transpired that "an ancient city of idolaters" in the Dra Valley, now in ruins, and called Ta-Punt by the natives, is also called *Anibna-Didoo* ("the town of Didoo"). It was pointed out that the traditions and beliefs of the people of that country had never been studied by anyone except by myself, and that we must seek there for that Cradle Land of the Egyptians, "the Holy Land of Punt," and not "somewhere on the shores of the Indian Ocean." A point of less importance, but of a good deal of interest, was also suggested to him, that evidence as to the existence of a dwarf race in the district of Akka, a country bounding to the South on the Sahara, had come to light.

As far back as 1883, a copy of a paper on "Mount Atlas and its Traditions," read at Montreal in 1882, was sent to Professor Sayce, and he was urged to spend a winter in Morocco and to look into the archaeology of that country.

For the first time, then, in November last I took part in investigations as to the dwarfs. As previous to that the enquiries were made by others and at a great distance from me, I may state what others have learned and know as to these dwarfs before giving an account of my enquiries and their results.

We have seen what was gleaned by Sir J. Drummond Hay's enquiries and also by those of Miss Day. The former has since then examined a native of Dra, as appears from his letter, which is given in the Preface.

The late Mr. Aissa Farar, a Colporteur, was visited at Beni Miskeen by a dwarf not over four feet high, who wished to buy an Arabic copy of the Gospels, and who, on being told the price, went away and returned with poultry, &c., equal in value to the price named, and on receiving the book kissed it reverently and hid it away in a fold of his dress, He was much more cordial and friendly than any of the Moors had been, a circumstance that lends some colour to the statements often made as to these dwarfs, that some of them are Christians. The dwarf said he came from a very wild and inaccessible country to the east-ward, where *his tribe lived* secluded from other people; and he told a curious story as to the creation of *a dwarf race*, and why the Creator allowed them to be so small, and so many other races so tall.

Mr. Farar was on a long excursion this summer in Northern Morocco, and was determined to find this little man, and get him to act as a guide to where his tribesmen live. I have but little doubt that he obtained some further information before he returned to Tangier. Arabic was his native language, so he had special advantages for seeing much of the natives. It is to be regretted very much that a fever (probably caught on his journey) proved fatal to him a few months ago. It is likely, however, that his family or friends may know what were the results of his enquiries as to these dwarfs.

The fourth person who made enquiries as to whether there was really a race of dwarfs as alleged, was Miss Herdman, at that time residing in Fez in connection with the Mission to the Berbers. Her abilities and knowledge of the Moors, and of their language and customs, are spoken most highly of by all who know her. Unfortunately, I had soon after writing to her, mentioned these dwarfs to a retired leader of a troop of acrobats, called Sidi Hamed O Moussa, and suggested to him that it would pay him to take a dwarf to England to be shown to scientific societies, and exhibited to the public. He professed never to have heard of such a race; and on my laughing and saying that I would find the dwarf, as there was one at Fez, he offered to write to him, which I did not wish him to do, as he would, no doubt, write forbidding the dwarf to be seen by Europeans. I wrote again to Miss Herdman, and told her she would probably not be able to get a sight of the dwarf. My anticipations were realized. In a few days he was at the point of death!

Her letter dated at Fez, Feb. 4th, 1891, says:—

There is a tribe of dwarfs inhabiting a part of Sus, called Oulad Sidi Hamed Ou Moussa, or Sedi Hamed ben Moussa. Some of them are acrobats, and come occasionally to Fez. They are expected in the spring. As the Court is at Morocco I think they are more likely, however, to go there, as there is more money going there. There is a man living at Fez of the tribe. I know persons who know him. Unfortunately he is too ill to leave his bed at present, I am told, and likely to die, having been ailing some time. They are about four feet high. *Various persons from Sus have described them to me,* and say that a woman is the size of an ordinary little girl, and a man with a beard is like a little boy. They are never called Akkas or any name but that which I have mentioned. Some are larger than others. Write to Morocco city, as they will be almost certain to be there for the festivities of the wedding of the Emperor's son.

You may rely on the information I have given you, as I have it from various sources. There are no dwarfs between Fez and Morocco, as far as I know. With kind regards, and ready to investigate anything for you and the interest of truth and science,

I remain, &c.,

Emma Herdman.

Our man-servant, a well-read Moor, did his
best to bring correct news. The dwarfs are said
to be rather expert thieves, for they climb on
each other's shoulders, and so scale high walls.
Others say that they can climb like cats without any foothold.

It will be seen that everybody that so far has described
them, agrees with Miss Herdman in her account of the
height of these dwarfs, who, with their distant kinsmen of
Equatorial Akka, are the smallest race in the world.

Mr. Walter B. Harris, the well-known traveller in Morocco, and author of "The Land of an African Sultan," whom
I met for a few minutes at Tangier in November last, told
me that he had seen a dwarf at Fez about four feet high,
and he promised to make enquiries as to this race, and to
get a photograph, if possible, of one of them.

The following extracts from a letter in the *Times* of Sept.
14th, 1891, are in accord with the preceding accounts of
these dwarfs:—

"Mr. E. G. Haliburton, in an interesting paper read before the Congress of Orientalists and reported in the *Times*
of Thursday, September 3, gives an account of the dwarf
tribes of Southern Morocco and Mount Atlas.

"I had the pleasure of meeting Mr. Haliburton in Morocco in November last, and of conversing with him on this
subject. I left Tangier the day after this conversation, and,
excepting for a short visit, did not find myself again in that
port until ten months later, at the end of August, when I left
for England, arriving ten days ago. This fact alone prevented

my communicating my notes to Mr. Haliburton on the subject before his paper was read, and, as I feel sure that the
existence of these hitherto almost unknown dwarfs will not
fail to interest the public, I take the liberty of writing to
your paper as the best means of adding a few additional
facts to Mr. Haliburton's most interesting account.

"The first time I chanced upon one of these dwarfs was
in the early months of 1887, in Fez, but except noticing
him as a peculiarly, nay remarkably, small man, it little
struck me that he might belong to a tribe uniform in stature. This man, by name 'Rebber, I afterwards became tolerably well acquainted with on several subsequent visits to
Fez, but in spite of my being on speaking terms with him I
found it difficult to persuade him to put aside his reserve
and speak freely of his people, and impossible to measure
him. However, I estimated his height at about 4 feet 2
inches. He is in, or past, middle life, the father of a family,
and the husband of a Moorish woman of normal size. The
fact that his children are the average height of the Arabs
and Moors of Fez might lead one to suppose, did I not know
positively to the contrary, that this dwarf is only a stray
case of undergrowth, and not coming of a dwarf people.
He is sharp in wit, lithe in limb, and most active, by no
means unskilled with the single-sticks, and a capital rider.
In colour he is a light dusky brown. He grows a short
scrubby grey-black beard. Until this year this much-petted
and well-known dwarf of Fez was the only specimen I had
chanced upon, but during this last spring fortune put another in my way, this time a younger man. As I was travelling in native costume, he seemed much less reserved and

suspicious than his fellow-tribesmen, and entered into conversation tolerably freely, though he again refused to be
measured or to allow me to take his photograph or measurements of his skill and limbs. *His tribe* he stated to be
Mahomedans, living in caves and tents in a range of mountains situated *to the southeast of Wad Draa*, but he did not
know the name 'Bani' applied to these mountains by Mr.
Haliburton, nor did he describe the Akkari, or inhabitants
of Akkar, as being dwarfs, though *a tribe of them is resident among them*. However, the evidence of Mr. Haliburton,
and the strange coincidence of Schweinfurth's Akka of
Central Africa leads me to discredit this statement, or rather,
perhaps, to believe that he was unaware that the name of
Akkari is used for the dwarfs as well as for a larger people.
He continued to say that his people are keepers of goats
and herds, and in their own country do but little manual
work, though one and all have some knowledge of trade,
such as tinkering and mending old shoes, &c., which they
practise should they migrate or travel from their native
lands. Arabic and Shleh are alike spoken by them, but I
could discover nothing of a distinctive language. They are
skilled, he said, in hunting ostriches, the feathers and eggs
of which they sell to the Arab traders of the Sahara. Their
country can be reached either by Tafilet, or Tafilelt, as it is
called by the Arabs and Berbers, or by Tarudant, in the
Soos Valley.

"Mr. Hunot also mentions that the natives of the Atlas
mountains are desirous of discovering the ancient treasure-
houses of the 'Romi,' as they call their predecessors in that
part. At Immintelleh, above Amsmiz, a small town situated

to the southwest of Morocco city and at the northern foot
of the Atlas, I was constantly questioned about a treasure-
house of the 'Christians,' said to exist at the bottom of a
curious deep pool, into which the water flowed by a sub-
terranean channel far beneath the surface. Of this spot I
gave a short description at one of the meetings of the Royal
Geographical Society ('Proceedings,' January, 1889). An
Akkari, or inhabitant of Akkar, I came across at Wazan, a
man by name Abdurrahman, who did not deny the existence of the dwarfs as so many do, either from ignorance or
superstition, but denied that the name Akkari applied to
them, stating, as did the second dwarf I interviewed, that
they were large people, as he himself was, but that *many of
the dwarfs were living amongst them, but that more still
inhabited the mountains to the south-east of Wad Draa.* In
questioning him as to ruins, &c., in the neighbourhood, he
mentioned to me the existence of a ruined and uninhabited
town, in good preservation, by name 'Osuru.' a name that
will no doubt interest Mr. Haliburton as being connected
with the worship of 'Didoo Osiri.' 'Osuru ' and 'Osiri' can
be easily explained to be one, owing to the probable omission of the two latter vowels in the Arabic spelling. This
Abdurrahman El Akkari is a man of medium height, light
brown in colour, of pleasing features; he is a worker and
mender of old shoes. He denied that the dwarfs are 'worshipped by the Moors,' and could in no ways explain the
extraordinary reticence of Mahomedans in speaking of
them. That they are supposed to bring good luck he frankly
acknowledged, and in taking advantage of this idea many
earn a livelihood by writing charms and telling fortunes.

The reverence that is paid them I believe to be merely the remains of a far older superstition than would exist in Mahomedan times."

Mr. Harris questions the idea as to these Barakers not being Moslems, but the evidence on this point is very strong. He also does not agree with Miss Herdman and a good many witnesses as to there being a tribe of acrobats.

"The Daggata, or 'black Jews,' are not in reality Jews, but are so classed by the Arab traders and slave dealers, just as other black tribes are classed as 'Christians'; I have come across many of these Daggata, who are easily recognizable by the three deep scars on their cheeks—a tribal mark. They are said by the other Soudan tribes to be cannibals, and are generally despised on this account, and on account of the general belief in their being Jews. As far as I could discover in conversation with such of them as I have met in slavery, and who had learned Arabic, they are pagans, but adopt Mahomedanism very readily.

"Mr. Haliburton again calls attention to Hanno's troglodytes. A large city of these strange cave dwellings I visited at Ain Torsil, in the Atlas Mountains, in 1887, and a somewhat full description written by myself was published in the *Times* of September 22nd of that year. I quite agree with Mr. Haliburton that these caves were the work of the dwarfs, the low ceilings, seldom over 5 feet 2 inches in height, alone going far to prove this theory.

"In another portion of his paper Mr. Haliburton mentions the 'haik' bearing the 'eye.' Does he not mean the Berber 's'lham' or 'bernous' of black woven goat hair, with the 'eye' in red and slightly decorated? The writer had one which he bought off the back of a Berber in the Atlas Mountains, for they are not by any means confined to the dwarf tribes, but are worn all through the Atlas Mountains. The theory that this 'eye' is the origin of the 'Cyclopes' is by no means far-fetched.

"It is to be hoped that if any reader possesses any knowledge of these dwarf tribes he will take this opportunity of putting it before the world, for with a collection of notes on the subject it would be far easier to follow up the study of one of the most interesting and least known races of the globe. With apologies for taking up so much of your valuable space,

"Believe me, Sir, your humble and obedient servant,

"Walter B. Harris."

We find on looking over the preceding accounts of this race of dwarfs, that they agree not only as to the main facts, but also as to details. Mr. Carleton, of Tangier, a nephew of the late Sir Wm. Kirby Green, tells me that he has seen three of these dwarfs, and has often talked with them. There are two dwarfs at Fez, one of them not much over 3 feet high. He was in Tangier for some months, and used to play chess with Mr. Carleton, who was then a boy. The dwarf is called Abdallah-ben-Saleh. He also saw the larger dwarf at Fez, and one near Alcazar, the shepherd of the Kaid of Ramoosh, who told him that he came from the district of Ouisda, in the country of the Beni Znassen, which cannot be very far from the French frontier.

The two following letters were received after I had handed in my paper on "Dwarfs and Dwarf Worship." The first, written at the Grosvenor Club, August 15th, is from Captain Rolleston, a well-known writer on Morocco, a country in which he has resided for many years:—

"Relative to your queries as to the dwarfs of Morocco, I saw one of them about six years ago, when residing at Tangier, He appeared to be about 35 to 40 years of age, between 3 feet and 4 feet high, and well proportioned. In colour he was no darker than an ordinary Spaniard, and, unlike the generality of the Moors, was clean shaven."

The next is from Mr. George Hunot, our Consul at Saffi, who has more than once, in recent works on Morocco, been pronounced the highest living authority on the Moors. His clerk, Mr. Harry Broome, a native of Mogador, had promised to get me a Shilhach version of an ancient poem on Karoun and the river Stoucha (Charon and the Styx). Stoucha is the name of a tribe, an extensive district, and also a river that flows into the ocean at Massa, and finds its way to Paradise.[2] Karoun, however, like Noah or Osiris (called Isiri), is also a divine instructor. God at his request gave him a plough, and he taught men agriculture, but wherever he went a woman followed him and undid his good work. She may perhaps be the original Pandora. Mr. Hunot also refers to some questions which I wished him to put to Dra people who attend the Saffi market, as to "an ancient city of idolaters" called Punt, or Ta-Punt. Mr. Hunot wrote to me from Saffi, August 8th, 1891:—

"With regard to the old song about Karoun and the Stoucha, I have been at Broome to get the man to have it translated into Arabic. My man does not know the song, but his friend, a Soos Taleb, does. It will yet reach you.

Broome is trying to get it, and I will urge him to forward it as soon as it is ready, and will assist also with the translation. I recollect the dwarf you allude to as living and dying at Mogador, and I think there is one also here at Saffi. The Mogador man was about the size of a boy of ten or eleven years of age. I do not think what you have found out is imaginary. I saw some Arab gipsies the other day—fortune-tellers; two or three of them were handsome-looking young women of about eighteen or nineteen. They were from the tribe of Oulad Bu Sebah ('Sons of the Father of Lions'). I know from experience that there are hundreds of names of places in the Atlas Mountains which we have never heard of. There are local names quite unknown to the natives living in the adjacent districts to those named. I hear from some of the natives that you must have got hold of valuable old chronicles belonging to the races of Europeans or 'Romi,' that they know once occupied their country. What they all want to know is where are the treasures and springs of water hidden by those races, who are believed to have had the power of the genii of that epoch? I am sorry you could not have the song ready for your visit to Cardiff. I should like to have Sir John's note to me, stating that important results had followed your researches."

Mr. Broome speaks of having often seen an old dwarf at Mogador, who lived there for many years, and was called Sidi Baraker, and, as a saint, was kissed on the shoulder by the Moors in passing him in the street. This superstitious reverence can hardly be wondered at when we remember Chénier's account of the Sultan's horse which had gone with Hadjis to Mecca, and was therefore sacred, the Sultan occasionally kissing the horse's tail and mane in the fervour of his reverence!

Considering how few of these dwarfs are to be found in Northern towns, it is surprising to note that so many Europeans have seen them, and that they all confirm the statements of natives as to the peculiar look, size, complexion, &c., of these dwarfs. I may mention, among those who have testified to the existence of these dwarfs, the evidence of Caillé (one of the few Europeans who ever travelled with a caravan from Timbuctoo to Dra, and reached that place alive), who endured an amount of hardships and ill-treatment that broke his health, and ultimately shortened his life.

He had never heard that a race of dwarfs south-east of Dra are slave-traders and ostrich hunters, who are so much alike that they cannot be distinguished from each other, and who go into the Sahara to meet caravans on their way from Timbuctoo, and to buy slaves and ostrich feathers, which they sell again in the markets of Sus. He noticed, as the caravan was approaching Akka, a dwarf who met them at a stopping place, and was long engaged with the leader of the caravan in business negotiations. The dwarf was left behind, but, to Caillé's surprise, reappeared at another stopping place, for Caillé supposed that the second dwarf was the same as the first. He very naturally remarked, "*ce petit homme m'apparaisait comme un nain mystérieux.*"

We have also the indirect testimony of Rohlfs, a renegade, who spoke Arabic imperfectly, and was robbed and left for dead by some of the lawless inhabitants of the River Dra. He did not go down the Dra Valley, but crossed the river far down on his way from Sus to Tafilelt, and must have been near a Baraker town, as he speaks of a place of some importance, being not far distant, called Zaouia Sidi Baraker (which he spells *Barca*). Although a renegade, he was looked on with suspicion as being a Christian, and the natives, therefore, would not have made the dwarfs a subject of conversation with him, for even among themselves they say little about them.

Had I never made any inquiries myself, the testimony of so many natives and Europeans, in so many different localities, all agreeing in their descriptions of this race, would be very strong evidence of there being tribes of such dwarfs in the southern districts of Morocco; the coincidence, too, that the Akkas of the Albert Nyanza are precisely similar to the little natives of Akka, south of Mount Atlas, is so remarkable, that, coupled with the evidence which I have referred to, it precludes the possibility of a mistake as to the existence of the Atlas dwarfs.

If, however, any doubt on the point exists, the confirmatory results of my own recent investigations, begun in Tangier in November, 1890, and concluded at Saffi in June, 1891, will be sufficient, I think, to settle it. Having unsuccessfully for two years tried to induce others to take up this subject, it was my duty to do my best to clear up the two points at issue, first, as to the existence of these dwarfs, and secondly, as to why so many Moors make such a mystery about them.

CONFIRMATORY INVESTIGATIONS
IN MOROCCO, 1890-91

The results of my inquiries at Tangier during the first few days of my stay there are described by me in a letter which has already been published.

"As a good deal of interest has been excited by the subject of the existence of a dwarf race within a few hundred miles of the Mediterranean, I may state for the information of winter migrants to Tangier that they can see a dwarf at that place, as he is always to be found near the gate of the large Soko. He is a donkey man, and is about 4 feet 6 inches in height; as tall as an Andaman Islander or Bushman, but six inches taller than an ordinary Atlas dwarf, and nearly a foot-and-a-half taller than Abdallah-ben-Saleh, the smaller of the two dwarfs that live at Fez. His comparatively large size is the result of his father, an Akka dwarf, having married a Moorish woman of ordinary size. Most of the following extracts from the beginning of my journal in Morocco, November, 1890, refer to him. Why the names of my Moorish informants are omitted is explained in the Preface.

"On arriving at Tangier, my first thought was to hunt up two natives who were there in 1887. They proved to be still there. One of them an Akkoui, a native of Akkairi, in Akka, and the other a Susi. When asked if they had ever heard of a race of small men, they at once replied that they had often seen dwarfs who inhabit Akka. The Akkoui said that *a town of them* was near Akkairi, and that 'they are called Taata Tajakants. They find money for people. They live at Akka-Igan, and are called Akka-Guil. Guil is the name of a place. They are about four feet high.' The Susi said that he had often seen them when in the Dra Valley, and that he had 'seen one that was not much over three feet in height.' They write on a wooden slate in order to find money."

The following is an entry in my journal a week later:—

"Having heard that there was a dwarf always about the Soko, I repeatedly asked the Akkoui and the Susi to bring him to me, and offered to pay them well for doing so; but they evidently had some reason for not letting me see him, as they never brought him to me. While walking to-day through the Soko (the market-place) with S. we saw the little man, who resembled an Akka. S. had previously offered him a job, but the dwarf did not turn up. We therefore hired his donkey, and he came with us to the International Hotel, and we induced him to come with us into a room there, but he was evidently in a great fright. He was very broad shoul-dered, and had a peculiar reddish complexion, good fea-tures, and long-shaped eyes, a little slanting up at the side like the Chinese eye. His expression was honest, intelli-gent, and good-humoured. I got him to let me mark his height on the wall, but he was in a tremor, evidently fear-ing the 'evil-eye.' He would not remove his fez; the edge of it was therefore included in taking his height. I made it four feet eight inches, but S. said that the dwarf raised his heels at least two inches. Therefore, allowing for the fez, we can make his height about four feet six inches. His name is Jachin-ben-Mahommed. He is thirty years of age, and a native of Wadnoon. His father is a native of Akka, and *one of the small race there*, and is, he says, much smaller than he himself is. Jachin is larger than any of his brothers or

sisters. His mother is an ordinary sized Moorish woma The
dwarfs, he says, are very brave and active, and great hunters
of ostriches, having small, swift horses that are called by a
name meaning 'those that drink the wind,' and that are fed
on dates and camels' milk, and are very lean, and, if judged
by their looks, would be set down as worthless. The dwarfs,
he says, are so active that one of them can jump over three
camels standing side by side. They wear a blue shirt embroidered on the breast and back, and have leggings that
come up nearly to the knee, and wear a haik with a large
yellow eye on its back. Their knife is different from those
used by the Moors. They put ground camels' flesh into a
bag when they travel. They weave cloth and make spinning wheels and spindles, which they sell. They go into the
Sahara to a fair, and buy slaves and ostrich feathers, and
bring them to the fair at Tazzawalt (a town near the sea,
about three days north of Wadnoon, where the tomb of Sidi
Hamed O Moussa is, and where the chief of the acrobats
reigns as a king). They are called Sahara people, and live
about eight days to the east of Wadnoon. They are about
four feet high, and attend the fairs in Sus, and are different
from the Moors, negroes, and mulattoes, as they have a
peculiar reddish complexion. They use firearms and sometimes bows and poisoned arrows.

"He said there is a man like himself in Tangier, and he
promised to bring him to me. I doubt his doing so, as the
Moors evidently have a dislike to having anything known
about these dwarfs. I subsequently told him I would give
him a new fez, but he never came for it. It will be seen that
he repeats almost *verbatim* the account given me of the

dwarfs by my Susi servant in 1888. (S.'s native language, as well as that of the manager of the hotel, who was present, is Arabic.) I used often to try to get Jachin to come to see me. He shaves his face, which is always taken as a sign that a man is not a true Moslem. The Ait Atta, who extend from Akka to Tafilelt, and are found to the east of Demnat, are said to have been once Christians. They shave their faces."

It is hard to imagine stronger evidence than that of a kinsman of the dwarfs, whose native place was on the borders of the Sahara, and who described a tribe of dwarf ostrich hunters. The criticism on it is very significant,—a quibble! I had remarked that the description of the ostrich hunters was precisely like that that had been previously given of them by my servant in Algeria in 1888. When I left that country he remained there. The critic quite gratuitously assumes a series of facts—that the Susi remained in my service; that I brought him with me to Tangier; that he was present at the examination; that he sat at the elbow of the dwarf; and that he suggested, and was allowed by us to suggest, unfounded statements to him; and that, therefore, the evidence of the dwarf was entitled to no weight! The *animus* of such criticism is so plain, that further comment on it is needless.

It will be noted that the ostrich hunters wear the *khanif* with "the all-seeing eye" on the back, a peculiar kind of *bournous* that is worn from Glaoua, near Morocco, to the Sahara, and from the Atlantic nearly to Tafilelt, by a majority of the population.

A Moor whose father was connected with the Emperor's army during its raid into Sus, says, "an Akka at Morocco lives on the funds of the Mosque of Sidi Abbas. There are others living there. I know two dwarfs at Fez. One is called Suldan El Baraka ('The Lord of Blessing'). I know two or three at Mequinez."

A native of Warzazat, in the Dra Valley, says that Taurirt in that district is a place where the small people live. *A tribe of small people* live at Garnata, and are called from its name Egarnan. A Moor, a native of Tafilelt (several days to Eastward of last-named place, says, "the little people live near the river Dora, near Tinzone in the Black Mountains, and trade with Tinzone. *There are more than a thousand there.* They shave their faces and the front of their head; colour reddish; lips something like those of a negro; but they are different from other people. They are about four feet."

It has come to light in the course of these investigations that the people of the Dra are known as Haratins, the Little and the Larger. The latter are the descendants of dwarfs, who have intermarried with black, or with white tribes. The first have a reddish-black complexion, and the latter a yellowish tint. It may be well to mention that Leo Africanus spells *Dra* "*Dara.*" In Smith's "Dictionary of Ancient Geography" we are told of the Daræ or Gætuli-Daræ, on the Steppes of the Great Atlas, and of "the Melano-Gætuli, a race from a mixture of the Gætuli and the Nigritians. The pure Gætulians were not an Ethiopic (negro), but a Libyan race, and were probably of Asiatic origin. They are supposed to have been the ancestors of the Berbers." The Haratin, according to De Foucauld, are looked down upon and are anxious to marry among the whites. When a man wishes to marry, the first question as to the lady is, with the Arabs, "*is she of an old family?*" with the Shilhach, "*has she money?*" and with a Haratin, "*is she white?*"

The first Haratin whom I saw was evidently not an ordinary Moor, and looked much more like an Englishman, and I asked him if he was not descended from an European. He brought to me the son of the governor of a district of Akka near Sus, of which Tazounin-Akka is the principal town, who said that "the Haratin are the tall and the short, the latter are living in three towns, Tamzrat, Atouayli, and Tadakoust; their faces are generally broad with a dark and yellowish complexion, their old language is forgotten, and is called *Tagnawot* or *Mizgitin*. They are constantly fighting with each other, and the governor has to make peace between them." He subsequently said, that "the little men are the oldest people. The Haratin who come from them are larger from intermarriages with other tribes. They speak the same language and are alike in looks and ways. They and the Zenegar also speak Hedah, Haidah or Tinker." He also said that Ait Wabili was one of the towns of the dwarfs. "*About 400 always there.* They are called Tajakant; another name is Aglimen. They make good dresses, and are fortune tellers, and know the stars well."

The Haratin was subsequently examined and said "the Ait Tinker, the Ait Souk, and Ait Sheltar, are near me, and there are *towns also of those names where there are little people*. We are called Haratin, Hartani, and Haidah or Heden. The whole country above Punt used to be called Heden. The Bani Mountains are called the mountains of the Christians, and are considered to belong to them. I do not think a Christian would be molested if he could get there. The Haiden, Haratin, or Tinker are different from the Zenegar, and know more than they do, but resemble them. We have a habit of mixing up words, and putting the ends of words first so that no one else can understand us."

A large Haratin (about five feet six inches in height), a native of Tamanart, one of the headquarters of the dwarfs, was next examined. He said there were the remains of ancient build-ings there, and that the following were the names of their towns in the Bani Mountains, a range bordering on the Sahara:— Asa, Atoumribet, Tashker-Yekn-ishet, and Bani-Youssi.

He refused to say anything when closely questioned as to the dwarfs. Asked who the Tinker were, he said "they are people who do not say all that they know."

When he first came into the room, he became very much excited when he was shown the frontispiece to Vol. I of Brugsch Bey's "Egypt under the Pharaohs," copied from the monuments, and representing the Rutennu offering tribute, and exclaimed "this is what we see at Tamanart"; but he afterwards denied that he had said this, and would say nothing more about the dwarfs and Tamanart. It has since transpired that the most interesting remains that survive in the Dra Valley, are at Tamanart, but what they consist of is not known to outsiders.

The next man that was examined was from the Sahara, a trader in dates, who spoke only Arabic and Fellatah. He was a stranger in Tangier, and could not find his way about the town. My servant, who spoke English and Arabic flu-ently, brought him to me. He said he had been at Ta Punt (called by the Arabs Tabount). There are a small modern town, and, two or three miles distant, the ruins of the old town, where there are "little figures, some with horse's heads, some with those of bulls. The people call them Ait Beni (!), Mahkerbu, and Ait Beni Hazor. Have heard them called *Patiki*. That is the name of the small people." After describing a remarkable feast called "the Night of Confusion," he said "the people from the Sahara have nothing to do with the feast. They go there to sell dates. The large Haratin are called Ait Brahim; the small, Ait Bar Hamed. The Haratin are the big and the small."

At Saffi, a man who had just arrived in the market-place with dates was examined. He described the old ruins near the town of Ta Punt. "There are many small figures there about eighteen inches or two feet high, but not of men. *They are mixed*, part men and part animals, some with the body of a man, and the head of a monkey or a dog. They are called *Ait Mahkerbu*. There are small and large Haratin. The small are about four feet high."

A Rabbi from Ternata, below Mezgita, on the Dra, was examined, and said "the Ait Atta are half Christians. The little people are not Moslems. Their feast is by themselves. It is supposed they worship Didoo-Isiri, but they keep to themselves. *There are many of them* near the Soudan. The Arabs fear them, and pay to be allowed to pass through their country. Their horses can do without water for four days, and are called *Dwiminagh* (they that drink the wind). They and the little people are the same. The Arabs call them *Baraker*. They are also called Ruhar."

Another Jew from Agadir was examined, and said "they call a dwarf Taleb el Elsir ('the little Taleb'). The Moors do not like to talk about them to strangers. *When they are in a town it is lucky.* Some of the small people do not like the Prophet Mahomed. *There are small people at Ait Tinker, called by that name.*"

Hearing that there were Hadjis in town at Tangier, I sent the mother of my servant (a Jewess from Mogador), to see if there was a dwarf among the Hadjis. She met a Moor among them whom she had known at Mogador, who told her that there were no dwarfs among them, for "most of the Barakers do not believe in the prophet, for their ancestors were Christians, so they seldom go to Mecca. They shave their faces like Christians."

Three men from the towns of Tazagora, Tatta, and Warzazat, said that at Ta Punt "there are some small figures with the heads of wolves and dogs, &c. They call them Beni Kerbu. Okillam is the name of the language of the Haratin." Another Draoui examined the day previously described these figures as "some were mixed, part animals and part men, about eighteen inches to two feet in height."

A native of Ait Psech, in Akka, says "there is a language called Tinker, which is a mixture of Shilhach topsy turvey. The Haratin speak it, also the Zeneghar." He said that at Ta Punt there are, in a ruined temple called *Abniat Didoo* ("the Temple of Didoo"[3]), "small figures inside the building, some eighteen inches, some three feet, very odd looking, no one can understand them. They are called Patiki; and so the little people are. The little men are very ugly, and have no eyebrows, and have smooth faces. People are afraid of them."

I also tried to examine a native of Sakiat Hamra ("The Red River"), a large black Saint, probably a Haratin, who,

as a diviner and fortune-teller, was all day long kept busy
in the Soko, telling people how to find stolen goods, &c.,
which he professed to do by writing columns of figures on
a wooden slate. When first asked to come to my hotel, he
said he did not care to have anything to do with either Christians or Jews; but he subsequently thought better of it, or
rather of the possible shilling, and came to see me. At first he
gave me information as to his country very freely, until he
was questioned about "the Little People," when he admitted reluctantly that there were *some hundreds of them* living
near the Sakiat Hamra, at four towns, named Toubold,
Oulad Kador, Oulad Haboub, and Moul Okaz; but when
pressed to give further information as to them, he became
very angry, and said that to do so would be against his religion!

A Haratin Saint of Zaouia Baraka, near Tamanart (the
place mentioned by Rohlfs) was examined. He had refused
some months previously, as he still did, to speak about the
dwarfs. He seemed surprised at my knowing that there were
dwarfs where he lived, and said, "how do you come to know
anything about them?" but he did not deny that they lived
near Zaouia Sidi Baraker, and Tamanart.

A Beni Bacchar from near Massa, said, "Iouzia or Idyl
is the name of the small people (four feet high), who live
in the mountains of Kaleez, in the country of Akka. The
small people worship Didoo Isiri, and they are the people
who let Didoo Isiri down and take him back with a rope."

Ali Ben Mohammed from Warzazat, said, "My tribe, the
Haratin, is the oldest people in the world, and all the gods
came from there. There is a saying for riches, 'you have all

the gold of Punt.' The story is, that in the olden time, there was a lot of gold and treasures, and it is all buried in Punt. The Mountain of the Christians (Jebel el Nasara), is in the country of Akka; near the bottom of the mountain is a town called Taskadeer, and near it there is another mountain called Ben Touhad. It is said that Christians were living there once. To the South of the town of Imini the short people live, and were Christians in the olden times; they live in the Valley of Imini, and are known by the name Imini." (He refused to speak further about the dwarfs, or to answer any questions. He said he did not know where the River Dra was!)

A man belonging to the tribe of Sidi Hamed Moussa, which he had disowned in consequence of some quarrel, was examined by Mr. Harry Broome, a native of Morocco, and said, "the name of the dwarf that died at Mogador nine or ten years ago, was Hadj Brahim Adousal, from the town of Tlata Wahaz, in the district of Ait Baha ou Dra. The name of the other dwarf was Aderdour, from Tifshrar. *Have seen many small men at Wadnoon. Adousal* is their name. *Hazora* also is the name of the small people. You cannot tell one from the other. *Some of the little people perform with the Sidi Hamed O Moussa.* One of them was sent to Saffi to reconcile me to my tribe, but did not succeed."

A native of Ait Seribu, Beni Amral, an Ait Atta, said, "at Idautanan, not far from Dra, there are people who put up a cross before them when they worship. They are whiter than the other people around them. The Ait Atta generally shave the face, as the small people do too. Those who shave their faces are called by the others Christians. There are dwarfs at Ahdeed, *in the Ait Messad, about* 1,500, *and about* 1,000 *at Ait Messal, also at Ait Bensid, but fewer, about* 500. We, the Ait Atta, do not reverence the small people very much, though when we meet one, and do not know his name, we call him Sidi Baraker. Haratin is the name of men, and Hartaniat of a woman."

Mohammed el Akoui, who belongs to that part of the Ait Atta who live in Akka, says his home is one day from Akairi, and that "there are *villages of the small people* near my country."

A native belonging to the Oulad Willal of Tafilelt said that "the Madid Sabaeen are neither Christians nor Mahommedans. The little men live near the River Dora, near the town of Tinzoni, which they trade with. They have hair like that of a negro. Their colour is reddish, and they are called Touwata. Iguilmim is *another tribe of small men*, near the sea, who are looked upon as saints. They are neither Christians nor Mahommedans."

A native of Warzazat said "many of the tribes of the Sahara have no religion, unless it be a worship of Didoo Isiri. The Zeneghar are not Moslems, but are people who sacrifice sheep."

In the steamer in which I came to England from Morocco, among my fellow passengers were two Jews who were natives of Mogador. There were also two Moors on board, one a merchant now living in Manchester. One of the Jews, a young man who has been living in Manchester for several years and speaks English fluently, said freely, without being questioned, that he had often seen the old Baraker that died at Mogador eight or ten years ago. "Have often heard of these dwarfs, and that they come from near *Ophiran* (spelled by Mardochée, *Ofaran*), but the Moors would not talk about them. 'God has sent them to us. We must not talk about them' they have said to me, when I wished to find out something about this race. The Moors worship the dwarfs, and are very superstitious about them."

The other Jew, a wealthy oil merchant, said that he remembered the dwarf at Mogador. "He was a great saint among the Moors." A Moor from Fez, a merchant, who was on his way to Manchester to reside there, said he knew two dwarfs at Fez very well, and that one of them was but little over three feet in height. He would not admit that the dwarfs are looked on as saints by the Moors.

A few days ago I called on a gentleman in the city, who is well known in connection with Morocco trade, and who said that he was a busy man, and had not had time to read what had appeared in the papers as to the Atlas dwarfs, but he said he had a Moorish servant, whom he would send to me. He however did not do so, but subsequently explained his neglect by the fact, that the Moor, when questioned, had proved very unsatisfactory, for the man, who is a native of Northern Morocco, when asked by him if he had ever heard of a small sized people in Morocco, said that there were tribes of them in the Atlas; but he added, "there is a saying among us about them, that *they have only one eye.*"[4] It therefore seemed useless to him to have any more conversation with the Moor on the subject.

The gentleman, in question, remembered that there was a clerk, a native of Mogador, in the office, and called him in, and asked him if he had ever heard of a race of dwarfs in Morocco. The clerk replied that he had often seen, several years ago, an old dwarf saint at Mogador, and had heard that there were tribes of such people somewhere in the Atlas.

The following is the statement of a Moor made October 1st, 1891, in presence of H. W. Bates, Esq., Assistant Secretary of the Royal Geographical Society:—

"I am thirty-two years of age; about seventeen years, as a seaman, I frequently visited England. I married in England; have been at Tazzawalt; I went there when I was nine years of age for a short visit. Have been at Mogador about four years. There are some small people in Haha, about four feet high; reddish people, different from others. They (the Dwarfs) are *Akka* people, but *it is not lucky to call them by that name. There are thousands of them to the South.* They call them Sidi Baraker. The people like to have them in towns, as they are lucky and bring good luck. Have seen them at Schedma, Terudant, and Tazzawalt; have been forward and backward, to and from Morocco. I often saw and spoke to an old Sidi Baraker who died at Mogador ten years ago. People passing him often kissed his hand or his shoulder. The Moors think it unlucky to talk about these Barakers. They tell you how to find money, and know more about the stars than other men. The Dra dwarfs are called Hartani or Haratin; also Jed-jedi ('The Fathers of our Fathers'); in Shilhach, *Jed-ibwa*."

When again examined by me he said, that "the outside people who perform with the Sidi Hamed O Moussa, do not belong to that tribe, who are acrobats 'from father to son.' There are dwarfs on the Dra. There must be *many thousands of these dwarfs altogether*. One of the ostrich

hunters used often to come to Mogador to sell ostrich feathers. He lived East of the Dra. Some of the dwarfs are shoe-
makers and good smiths. They know more about the stars
and hidden treasures than other men."

Footnotes

[1] The Lesser Atlas divides Akka from Sus, but there are several roads
through passes, which connect them.

[2] Rabbi Mardochée, when he reached the extensive district of Stoucha
entered a vast forest "called after a man of the name of *Himmou
Karroûm*," (See *Bulletin de Géog.*, x, 565.)

[3] This has been since singularly confirmed by my meeting with the
description by Scylax of a similar temple, South of Mount Atlas,
with representations of animals and men on its altar, which was
built by *Dædalus* (Didoo?). There must, however, be many such
ruins in that country, for Rabbi Mardochée met near Wadnoon
with wonderful ancient remains, a high wall connecting two mountains and guarded by towers, old temples, and stones inscribed
with figures of men and animals. It is a pity his journal has not
been published. (See *Bulletin de Géog. Décr.* 1875).

[4] See Mr. W. B. Harris' letter in Preface. The Nubians apply the same
myth to the Akkas of Equatorial Africa, see "Heart of Africa," II,
123.

Dwarf Races and Dwarf Worship

R. G. Haliburton

The following consists of portions of my paper read before the Oriental Congress, which appeared in the *Times* of September 3rd, 1891. The parts which referred to early dwarf races in America and the West Indies were not reported, nor that portion which traced the wide spread belief in the Old World, and in the New, that the first Creation produced only monstrous or malformed mortals, to the existence of early dwarf races. The evidence which was relied on as to the existence of dwarfs in the Atlas, and which was submitted in MSS. to the Congress, is now printed for the use of those who may be interested in the subject.

The singular, and at first sight incredible, fact, that the existence of a race of dwarfs, under four feet high, in the Atlas Mountains, only a few hundred miles from the Mediterranean, has for 3,000 years at least been kept a profound secret by the natives, was first brought to the notice of the scientific world by a paper of mine, read in my absence, at the Bath meeting of the British Association in 1888. The information which had been collected by me was confirmed by that subsequently obtained at Tlemçen, Algeria, by Miss Day, and at Tangier by the Right Hon. Sir John Drummond Hay; but it seemed prudent to defer publishing the paper until the point could be cleared up—why do so many of the Moors dread strangers knowing about this pygmy race?

After a lapse of two years I was able to visit that country early in November last, and remained until June 10, seven months in all, and during that period managed to collect very conclusive evidence both from natives and from Europeans who resided in that country.

In Equatorial Africa it has been observed with interest that the larger races near the dwarfs resemble them in colour. In the Dra Valley, South of Mount Atlas, the dwarfs are called "the Little Haratin." "The Large Haratin" (or, more properly, "the Larger"), who were known to the ancients as the Melano-Gætuli, or the Gætuli-Daræ, i.e., Dra-Gætulians, have a reddish-black complexion from intermarriages between the dwarfs and a Nigritian race, or a yellowish colour from a cross between the dwarfs and light coloured tribes.

The larger Haratin are generally about five feet high, though many tall men among them are to be found. In Sus, which lies between the ocean and Dra and Akka, the dwarfs are called Aglimen, and their offshoots are rather a small race with a light red complexion, a tribe of acrobats called Ait Sidi Hamed O Moussa ("the tribe of our Lord Hamed, the son of Moses"), with whom the dwarfs perform in Southern Morocco, avoiding the coast towns where Europeans are.

These acrobats from Morocco, who are smiths and tinkers, are, according to Brugsch Bey ("Egypt under the Pharoahs," vol. I, p. 5), represented on the monuments of the Fourth Dynasty as performing in Egypt! How long previously they had been known to the Egyptians cannot be conjectured. No doubt centuries, perhaps thousands of years, nor is it likely that they limited their wanderings to Egypt. They probably found their way to the Southern and Northern shores of the Mediterranean. Troy then did not exist. The Greeks were savages.

The Sidi Hamed O Moussa, who is referred to by Mr. Hunot, told me an amusing story of an unprofitable performance of his troupe near a village of Daggata (Black Jews), not far from Timbuctoo. The acrobats were surprised at nobody coming to see their performance. But they were still more surprised when they discovered that the whole population of the place had run away, believing that the acrobats were jins and imps who were amusing themselves. This will show what a profound impression must have been made by these acrobats, if they found their way to Greece at the remote period when they were depicted on the monuments of Egypt.

The dwarfs of Mount Atlas are called *Patiki* ("ancestors"), Pati or Pata meaning a "father," and may be the dwarfs whose grotesque images were called by the same name— Patæki, and the Cabeiric worship of which may have been an importation from the Phoenician colonies south of Mount Atlas.

It is worthy of note that the scenes of nearly all the earliest myths of Greece are laid in Mount Atlas (called by

the natives Ida-na-Dauran or Ida-Dran—*i.e.*, Mount Tau-
rus), or in the Island of Crete, the first landing place for
immigrants from Libya. Many are the traces of that migration in Crete and its myths. For instance, Ida is a not a Greek
but a Shilhach word, the equivalent of the Latin *Mons*. There
are scores of Idas in Southern Morocco, though few, if any,
north of the Great Atlas. The Greeks may have mistaken
the Shilhach word for a "mountain" for a name, and thus
have made their mythology centre in Mount Ida—*i.e.*,
Mount Mons. The caves at its base became the workshops
of mysterious cave dwellers, who established there their
magic forges, and were called Idæi Dactyli;[1] and were so
revered that they were included among the great gods, the
Cabeiri, sometimes called in Greek Apatæki. It is somewhat
startling, in this late age, to meet south of Mount Atlas with
original versions of familiar Greek myths. We may from
many others select one which was a very notable one among
mythologists. Mohammed-ben-Ibrahim, a Beni Bacchar, of
Massa in Sus, says, "Theba is to the east of Paradise Mountain" (a hill near the source of the river Did). "It was built
originally by Kadmon; Kadmon is the man who bought the
ground by the size of a cow's skin, and who brought people
in boxes to Ta-Punt, and took others back. He was in the
habit of hiding the cows under the ground."

Probably on both sides of the Atlantic the ancient dwellings cut in cliffs were made by dwarfs. The little race to
the west of "the sandy ridge" south of the Atlas, who captured the Nasimonian explorers, are called by Herodotus
Troglodytes. The cliffs of the Atlas Mountains are frequently dotted with cave dwellings which must have been

used by a small race, as they are not more than five feet
high. They are now no longer used, though I am told some
of these dwarfs on the river Dora, or Didoo, in the Bani
Mountains, near Tinzone, are still Troglodytes. They were
probably the tribe of dwarfs which ancient writers say
owned a remarkably small breed of horses. The ponies of
the dwarfs near the Sahara are famed for their endurance
and speed, and are therefore used by them in hunting ostriches.
Rabbi Juda, a Shilhach Jew, of Ternata, in the Dra Valley,
says, "the little people are not Moslems. It is supposed that
they worship Didoo Isiri. They keep their feast by themselves. There are many of them near the Soudan; the Arabs
fear them and pay to be allowed to pass through their country." "Their horses can do without water for four days, and
are called dwiminagh (they that drink the wind)."

The dwarfs are very holy men, though they shave their
faces, and do not love the Prophet as much as they should.
Some say that they are Christians; others assert that they
are idolaters and "worship Didoo Isiri." Sometimes I had
little difficulty in getting the Moors to speak of them, though
they have exclaimed with surprise, "How do you come to know
anything about them?" But superstitious natives, and especially the Haratin living near Tamanart in the Dra Valley,
have often cut short the conversation on my pressing them
to tell me as to the numbers and place of residence of the
dwarfs, &c. One said, "It is a sin to speak about them to
you. I shall say nothing." Others say, "God has sent them
to us. We must not talk about them." A young Jew now
living in Manchester, but a native of Mogador, said that
the Moors worshipped these Barakers, and would not talk

freely about them to the Jews. He had tried to find out about them, but without success. He had constantly, when a boy, seen an old Baraker who died at Mogador about eight or ten years ago, and who was looked on as a great Saint, and as such was kissed on the shoulders by the Moors as they passed him in the street. These dwarfs are supposed to bring good luck to the towns where they reside, and are guardians and protectors, resembling in this respect the Palladium of the Trojans. If strangers were to succeed in carrying them out of the country, good luck would depart with them. It is probable that some such superstitious belief was at the bottom of the difficulty which puzzled and baffled Schweinfurth in his attempt to get a sight of the dwarf Akkas of the Monbutto country, the king of which sent away by night his regiment of dwarfs, so as to keep them out of the way of his visitor.

In Europe and Britain the dwarfs of early ages are remembered as smiths, artificers, and magicians, but no one has conjectured where they can have come from. If the Dra was, as it is believed by some to have been, a great prehistoric work-shop, the Birmingham of the Bronze Age, the problem could be easily settled. The little and the larger Haratin are still great workers in metal, magicians and potent doctors, whose staple remedy seems to be safe if not sure. They make little books which are carried about as charms or are placed in water, which has marvellous virtues that can cure all the ills that flesh is heir to. Wherever the Haratin went they must have "astonished the natives," as they wear a peculiar haik, which has a large eye on its back, about a yard in length. It is probable that the earliest traditions of

Greece described wandering bands of masons and smiths as "the men with the eye," which in time may have become "the men with only one eye"—the Cyclopes. A *khanif* such as they wear is now in my possession. The skill of the modern Cyclops is devoted to sinking deep wells. The well-sinkers of Morocco come from the Dra to the cities North of the Atlas, and are still to be seen wearing their Cyclopean haik.[2] In Northern Morocco there is a belief that there is under the ground a race of little men who can be heard at work. Two centuries ago it was said that this belief existed also in Wales. "Robert Kirk, minister of Aberfoyle," in his work published in 1691 on "The Secret Commonwealth," which treats exhaustively of "the subterranean people," their appearance, habits, dwellings, &c., says (p. 14), "Even English authors relate of Barry Island, in Glamorganshire, that laying your ear unto a clift of the rocks, blowing of bellows, striking of hammers, clashing of armour, filing of iron, will be heard distinctly ever since Merlin enchanted those subterranean wights to a solid forging of arms for Aurelius Ambrosius and his Britons, till he returned. Which Merlin being killed in battell, and not coming to loose the knot, those active Vulcans are ty'd to a perpetual labour." The mention of these little Vulcans reminds us that the father of the gods, the oldest of all, Vulcan or Patah, the eighth of the earliest system of Egyptian deities, was a Patæcus, and was represented as a dwarf. Classical mythology has made Vulcan lame and deformed, while his workmen "the seven Cyclopes," were supposed to represent the earliest race of men, those progenitors of mankind whom the Hindoos worship as the Pitris. If he, the greatest, was a dwarf, the other seven must also have been dwarfs. What a beginning for the Gods of antiquity—seven dwarf masons with their Pygmy master-mason! Well may the Haratin boast, as their ancestors, the old Atlantes, did, that they are the oldest people in the world, and that all other nations got their gods from them.

The following additional notes may be of interest:—

Professor Sayce in his excellent note on Herodotus, B. III, Ch. 37, says, that Ptah is represented as a dwarf (see also Rawlinson's and Kenrick's notes); and Egyptologists admit, that the oldest type of the Divinity in Egypt was that of *Ptah*, "the Creator" (identified by the Greeks with their Hephaistos, "the Architect of the Universe").

He also points out, what I think is a new idea, that from the name Ptah, or Patah, is derived that of *Patæki*; and that those little known groups of divinities called Patæki or Cabeiri were sometimes classed together. But there is a confirmation of his view of the connection of names between Patah and Patæki in the remarkable fact, that *Patah and the Patæki were dwarfs*. Nor was this earliest form of the Godhead, the deification of Pygmies, confined to Egypt, for Selden says that all the greatest gods of Palestine and Syria were *Patæki*, and he shows that little images of them were supposed to bring safety and good luck, and were placed on prows of ships by the Phoenicians, while the presiding Genius and protector of the banquet table of the Greeks was an image of a Pygmy Hercules.

Probably in Rome they were the venerated Penates, who were classed among the Cabeiri, and were household gods which, under different names, were worshipped among so many nations of antiquity. It was, perhaps, a feeling that it was unlucky to speak of these Pygmy Deities, that has thrown a cloud of mystery over the Cabiric Divinities of antiquity. Movers, in the first chapter of his Phönizier, says that that group of deities called Dactyls, Cabiri, Corybantes, and Cyclopes, were similar to those old Germanic divinities now known as Kobolds. I had not read this passage when I suggested that they were like our Fairies and Brownies. The Monbuttoo regard the Akkas "as a sort of benevolent spirits or mandrakes who are in no way detrimental." (See "Heart of Africa," ii, 145.) A reference to Mr. MacRitchie's interesting little work, "The Testimony of Tradition" (Paul, Trench, and Co., 1890), pp. 131-137, shows that the memory of a dwarf race of smiths was once reverenced by the Irish, whose old "God of the Bru of the Boyne," seems to have been a Vulcan.

The seven companions of Vulcan, his masons or workmen, the Seven Cyclopes, who, as we have seen, are included among the dwarf Patæki, derived their name from their having had only one eye each. The same myth is related about the Arimaspi, and they too, strange to say, were workers in metals or a mining race; and is still told, as we have seen, of the dwarfs both of Equatorial Akka and of Akka in the Southern Atlas. Writers on the Isle of Man and the Highlands seem to agree that the Fairies represent an extinct dwarf race. Mr. MacRitchie seeks for existing representatives of it among the Eskimo, Laplanders, and even the distant Ainos. It is possible that we may find some survivals of this race of dwarfs without going as far North as the Arctic regions, or as far South as the Albert Nyanza or the Congo.

We need not regard with incredulity, or "with a disdainful smile," the veneration of the Moors and of the Monbuttoo for these dwarfs, for the very same superstition still exists among some of our peasantry, though it is now between one and two thousand years, at least, since the dwarf race in Britain died out, and was represented by "the Little People," that haunt the fairy "brows," or mounds of Wales and Ireland. "I am a Welshman," writes Professor Sayce, September 27th, "and was brought up in a Welsh village, so I know that the Kelts do not like to mention the fairies. My own nurse's brother had been carried off to fairy-land for a year. Do not forget that the Basques have a Cyclops myth of the one-eyed Tartaroa. You will find the picture of a dwarf from the 12th Dynasty Tombs of Beni-Hassen, given in Wilkinson's "Ancient Egyptians" (Birch's Edition), ii, 70."

If any practical joker were to visit (after due notice of his coming and its professed object), all the "fairy mounds" in secluded districts in Wales and Ireland, and were to pretend to go through a form of exorcising and banishing "the Good People" from their ancient homes, he would create a storm among the peasantry that would rather astonish him.

FOOTNOTES

[1] The name *Dactyl* (literally "a finger"), may have meant a "dwarf," and have been a synonym of *Pygmy* (literally "a fist"). Our phrase is "a Hop o' my Thumb."

[2] Dr. Oliver says that the "all-seeing eye " is a *Masonic* symbol!

Dwarfs and Dwarf Worship

Letter to the Editor (*London Times*), Sept. 14, 1891

R. G. Haliburton

To the Editor of the *Times*.

Sir,—As a good deal of interest has been excited by the subject of the existence of a dwarf race within a few hundred miles of the Mediterranean, I may state for the information of winter migrants to Tangier that they can see a dwarf at that place, as he is always to be found near the gate of the large Soko. He is a donkey man, and is about 4ft. 6in. in height; smaller than an Andaman Islander or Bushmen, but 6in. larger than an ordinary Atlas dwarf, and nearly a foot and a-half larger than Abdallah-ben-Saleh, the smaller of the two dwarfs that live at Fez. His comparatively large size is the result of his father, an Akka dwarf, having married a Moorish woman of ordinary size. Most of the following extracts from the beginning of my journal in Morocco, November, 1890, refer to him. The names of my Moorish informants are omitted, as I do not wish to get them into trouble with other Moors:—

"On arriving at my hotel my first thought was to hunt up two servants who were there in 1887. They proved to be still there. One of them an Akkoui, a native of Akkairi, in Akka, and the other a Susi. When asked if they had ever

77

heard of a race of small men, they at once replied that they had often seen dwarfs who inhabit Akka. The Akkoui said that a town of them was near Akkairi, and that 'they are called Taata Tajakants. They find money for people. They live at Akka-Igan, and are called Akka-Guil. Guil is the name of a place. They are about 4ft. high.' The Susi said that he had often seen them when in the Dra Valley, and that he had 'seen one that was not much over 3ft. in height. They write on a wooden slate in order to find money.'"

The following is an entry in my journal a week later:—

"Having heard that there was a dwarf always about the Soko, I repeatedly asked the Akkoui and the Susi to bring him to me, and offered to pay them well for doing so; but they evidently had some reason for not letting me see him as they never brought him to me. While walking to-day through the Soko (the market-place) with S. we saw the little man, who resembled an Akka. S. had previously offered him a job, but the dwarf did not turn up. We therefore hired his donkey, and he came with us to the International Hotel, and we induced him to come with us into a room there, but he was evidently in a great fright. He was very broad shouldered, and had a peculiar reddish complexion, good features, and long-shaped eyes, a little slanting up at the side like the Chinese eye. His expression was honest, intelligent, and good humoured. I got him to let me mark his height on the wall, but he was in a tremor, evidently fearing the 'evil eye.' He would not remove his fez; the edge of it was there-fore included in taking his height. I made it 4ft. 8in., but S. said that the dwarf raised his heels at least two inches. Therefore, allowing for the fez, we can make his height

about 4ft. 6in. His name is Jachin-ben-Mahommed. He is
30 years of age, and a native of Wadnoon. His father is a
native of Akka, and one of the small race there and is, he
says, much smaller than he himself is. Nachin is larger than
any of his brothers or sisters. His mother is an ordinary-
sized Moorish woman. The dwarfs, he says, are very brave
and active, and great hunters of ostriches, having small,
swift horses that are called by a name meaning 'those that
drink the wind,' and that are fed on dates and camels' milk,
and are very lean, and, if judged by their looks, would be
set down as worthless. The dwarfs, he says, are so active
that one of them can jump over three camels standing side
by side. They wear a blue shirt embroidered on the breast
and back, and have leggings that come up nearly to the knee,
and wear a haik with a large yellow eye on its back. Their
knife is different from those used by the Moors. They put
ground camels' flesh into a bag when they travel. They
weave cloth and make spinning wheels and spindles, which
they sell. They go into the Sahara to a fair, and buy slaves
and ostrich feathers, and bring them to the fair at Tazzawalt
(a town near the sea, about three days north of Wadnoon,
where the tomb of Sidi Hamed O Moussa is, and where the
chief of the acrobats reigns as a king). They are called Sahara
people, and live about eight days to the east of Wadnoon.
They are about 4ft. high, and attend the fairs in Sus, and
are different from the Moors, negroes, and mulattoes, as
they have a peculiar reddish complexion. They use firearms and sometimes bows and poisoned arrows. He said
that there is a man like himself in Tangier, and he promised to bring him to me. I doubt his doing so, as the Moors

evidently have a dislike to having anything known about these dwarfs. I subsequently told him I would give him a new fez, but he never came for it. It will be seen that he repeats almost *verbatim* the account given me of the dwarfs by my servant in 1888. (S.'s native language, as well as that of the manager of the hotel, who was present, is Arabic.) I used often to try to get Jachin to come to see me. He shaves his face, which is always taken as a sign that a man is not a true Moslem. The Ait Atta, who extend from Akka to Tafilelt, and are found to the east of Demnat, are said to have been once Christians. They shave their faces."

Jachin's account of his kinsmen and their ponies also agrees with that of the Rabbi from Ternata, which is given in the report of my paper in *The Times* of Thursday last. Caillé did not know of a race of dwarfs in Akka who were all so alike that a stranger could not distinguish one from the other, nor did he know that they go into the Sahara to meet caravans and to buy slaves and ostrich feathers, to be sold afterwards in Sus. When his caravan approached Akka he saw a dwarf who was busily engaged in business negotiations with the leader of the caravan. When he arrived at the next station, to his surprise, he saw, apparently, the very same dwarf that had been left behind at the previous stopping place. Naturally enough he terms this ubiquitous personage "a mysterious dwarf." This mistake on his part is an indirect proof of the authenticity of his work.

The son of a Moorish official, who accompanied the army in its recent raid into Sus, says, "A dwarf in the city of Morocco lives on the funds of the mosque of Sidi Abbas. There are others living there. I know two dwarfs at Fez.

One is called Suldan-el-Baraker ('the Lord of Blessing'). I also know two or three at Mequinez."

One of these Fez dwarfs is but little over 3ft. in height, and is called Abdallah-ben-Saleh. He is probably the dwarf whom Captain Rolleston saw in 1885 at the oil market at Tangier. The dwarfs at Fez and at Alcazan are the only ones in northern cities now living who have been seen by Europeans. One who came from the east of Demnat was seen by Mr. Aissa Farar at Beni Misquien. The one at Alcazan, who is shepherd to the Kaid of Ramoosh, told Mr. Carleton that he came from the country of the Beni Zniessen, near the French frontier.

My six European informants have resided some years, most of them many, in Morocco, and two of them, Messrs. Carleton and H. Broome, are natives of that country; while Mr. Hunot has been many years Consul at Saffi, and is recognized as the highest authority on Morocco and the Moors. As no person of ordinary intelligence can be mistaken as to the fact of his having a dwarf under 4ft. high, these persons when they stated that they had each seen one or more of these dwarfs must have spoken the truth, or must have deliberately invented an untruth—a somewhat cruel conclusion which even the most cautious critic would hesitate to assume *ex abundanti cautelâ*. Negative evidence, which is generally unsatisfactory, is in this case almost worthless, for scores of Englishmen might very honestly assert that they had lived north of the Great Atlas for years, and yet that they had never seen or heard of a dwarf. The fact that the dwarfs, excepting half-a-dozen or so, live not only out of the reach of Europeans, but also out of the limits of the Sultan's rule, is a sufficient explanation for this, coupled as it is with a superstitious reticence as to this race on the part of the Moors.

Any one who goes to Morocco as a tourist is hardly likely to pick up much information as to these dwarfs, now that strangers are prying into that subject. Before I left Tangier I had to give up my inquiries there as to the races and antiquities of the Southern Atlas, as some of my informants were warned by other Moors to avoid giving any information to Christians. The same thing occurred in 1887. Of course, an unfriendly hint to the Moors from some Europeans would account for this; but there does not seem to be any reason why this should have taken place, as the subjects I have been inquiring into are of little interest to European residents in that country.

I should strongly advise European travellers or tourists not to try to visit the isolated districts inhabited by this race, as they would in all probability be murdered or robbed by lawless tribes, who plunder or murder strangers, whether Moslems, Jews, or Christians. In two districts Jews are murdered and their goods are scattered about, no one being willing to use anything that has belonged to a Jew.

I remain obediently yours,

R. G. Haliburton

Dwarfs and Dwarf Worship

Letter to the Editor (*London Times*), September 14, 1891

Walter B. Harris

To the Editor of the *Times*

Sir,—Mr. R. G. Haliburton, in an interesting paper, read before the Congress of Orientalists and reported in *The Times* of Thursday, September 3, gives an account of the dwarf tribes of southern Morocco and Mount Atlas.

I had the pleasure of meeting Mr. Haliburton in Morocco in November last, and of conversing with him on this subject. I left Tangier the day after this conversation, and, excepting for a short visit, did not find myself again in that port until ten months later, at the end of August, when I left for England, arriving ten days ago, This fact alone prevented my communicating any notes to Mr. Haliburton on the subject before his paper was read, and, as I feel sure that the existence of these hereto almost unknown dwarfs will not fail to interest the public, I take the liberty of writing to your paper as the best means of adding a few additional facts to Mr. Haliburton's most interesting account.

The first time I chanced upon one of these dwarfs was in the early months of 1887, in Fez, but except noticing him as a peculiarly, nay remarkably, small man, it little struck me that he might belong to a tribe uniform in stature. This

man, by name 'Rebber, I afterwards became tolerably well
acquainted with on several subsequent visits to Fez, but in
spite of my being on speaking terms with him I found it
difficult to persuade him to put aside his reserve and speak
freely of his people, and impossible to measure him. However, I estimated his height at about 4ft. 2in. He is in, or
past, middle life, the father of a family, and the husband of
a Moorish woman of normal size. The fact that his children
are the average height of the Arabs and Moors of Fez might
lead one to suppose, did I not know positively to the contrary, that this dwarf is only a stray case of undergrowth,
and not coming of a dwarf people. He is sharp in wit, lithe
of limb, and most active, by no means unskilled with the
single-sticks, and a capital rider. In colour he is a light
dusky brown. He grows a short scrubby gray-black beard.
Until this year this much-petted and well-known dwarf of
Fez was the only specimen I had chanced upon, but during
this last spring fortune put another in my way, this time a
younger man. As I was travelling in native costume, he
seemed much less reserved and suspicious than his fellow-
tribesmen, and entered into conversation tolerably freely,
though he again refused to be measured or to allow me to
take his photograph or measurements of his skull and limbs.
His tribe he stated to be Mahomedans, living in caves and
tents in a range of mountains situated to the south-east of
Wad Draa, but he did not know the name "Bani" applied to
these mountains by Mr. Haliburton, nor did he describe the
Akkari, or inhabitants of Akkar, as being dwarfs, though a
tribe of them is resident among them. However, the evidence of Mr. Haliburton and the strange coincidence of

Schweinfurth's Akka of Central Africa makes me to discredit this statement, or rather, perhaps, to believe that he was unaware that the name Akkari is used for the dwarfs as well as for a larger people. He continued to say that his people are keepers of goats and herds, and in their own country do but little manual work, though one and all have some knowledge of trade, such as tinkering and mending old shoes, &c., which they practise should they migrate or travel from their native lands. Arabic and Shleh are alike spoken by them, but I could discover nothing of a distinctive language. They are skilled, he said, in hunting ostriches, the feathers and eggs of which they sell to the Arab traders of the Sahara. Their country can be reached either by Tafilet, or Tafilelt, as it is called by the Arabs and Berbers, or by Tarudant, in the Soos Valley.

Mr. Haliburton, in quoting a letter written by Mr. Hunot to Captain Rolleston, speaks of the "Oulad bu Sebah"— "sons of the father of lions." This curious tribe is not confined to the Soos district, but are also to be found in Shiedma, in Gibel Hadid, between Saffi, on the coast, and Morocco city, and again there is a colony of them inhabiting a large village between the Karias of Remoosh and Hurbasseh, on the road to Fez, about 80 miles south of Tangier. These latter, however, have lost any distinctive sign of their tribe, and no doubt it is long since that they left their native soil, as a large pile of rock in the immediate neighbourhood of their village is known as "Hajra bu Sebah." However, those on Gibel Hadid still retain many of their gipsy qualities, and in most cases still allow their hair to grow long, like the Aissoua and one or two other religions sects. A considerable amount of respect is shown to them by the Moors and Arabs, although they are not "Shorfa," or descendants of the Prophet. These people are of medium stature, and speak Arabic and Shleh.

Mr. Hunot also mentions that the natives of the Atlas mountains are desirous of discovering the ancient treasure-houses of the "Romi," as they call their predecessors in that part. At Immintelleh, above Amsmiz, a small town situated to the southwest of Morocco city and at the northern foot of the Atlas, I was constantly questioned about a treasure-house of the "Christians," said to exist at the bottom of a curious deep pool, into which the water flowed by a sub-terranean channel far beneath the surface. Of this spot I gave a short description at one of the meetings of the Royal Geographical Society ("Proceedings," January, 1889). An Akkari, or inhabitant of Akkar, I came across at Wazan, a man by name Abdurrahman, who did not deny the exist-ence of the dwarfs as so many do, either from ignorance or superstition, but denied that the name Akkari applied to them, stating, as did the second dwarf I interviewed, that they were large people, as he himself was, but that many of the dwarfs were living amongst them, but that more still inhabited the mountains to the south-east of Wad Draa. In questioning him as to ruins, &c., in the neighbourhood he mentioned to me the existence of a ruined and uninhabited town, in good preservation, by name "Osuru," a name that will no doubt interest Mr. Haliburton as being connected with the worship of "Didoo Osiri." "Osuru" and "Osiri" can be easily explained to be one, owing to the probable omission of the two latter vowels in the Arabic spelling.

This Abdurrah-man El Akkari is a man of medium height, light brown in colour, of pleasing features; he is a worker and mender of old shoes. He denied that the dwarfs are "worshipped" by the Moors, and could in no ways explain the extraordinary reticence of Mahomedans in speaking of them. That they are supposed to bring good luck he frankly acknowledged, and in taking advantage of this idea many earn a livelihood by writing charms and telling fortunes. The reverence that is paid them I believe to be merely the remains of a far older superstition than would exist in Mahomedan times. On one point I cannot agree with Mr. Haliburton—viz., as to their religion. I have never heard them spoken of as anything but Mahomedans, nor would their existence as infidels be possible surrounded on all sides as they are by the most fanatical of Mahomedan tribes. The evidence of Mr. Haliburton himself tells against his theory of their having another religion, for he has several times heard them spoken of as "Sidi baraka." "Sidi," a word meaning "my lord," is never used by Mahomedans to infidels, while the word "baraka" is peculiarly a religious expression of Mahomedanism, as implying the direct influence of God, and certainly would never issue from the lips of a Mahomedan in speaking of any one of a different religion. So sacred is the expression that amongst the Moors and Arabs it is used only as a title of the Sultan, or of the greater Shorfa, or descendants of the prophet Mahomed.

Sidi Hamed O Moussa is, as Mr. Haliburton implies, the patron saint of the Soosi acrobats, but I do not think the expression ait or oulad (sons of) Sidi Hamed O Moussa can be used of a tribe; in this case I infer that it implies more the devotees of rather than the absolute family. I entertained this year for a night a troup of these jugglers in my camp, and though all passing under the name of Oulad Sidi Hamed O Moussa, they were from different parts of Morocco. Thus I think that the name implies the devotees of the "saint," just as the names Aissoua and Hamacha imply the devotees of Sidi Ben Aissa of Mequinez and Sidi Ali Ben Hamdouch of the Zarahoun. One of the troup I entertained caused me no little astonishment by speaking in five European languages, and telling me he had performed in the Alhambra in Leicester-square. The tomb of Sidi Hamed O Moussa is situated two days' journey from Tarudant, in the Soos valley.

The Daggata, or "black Jews," are not in reality Jews, but are so classed by the Arab traders and slave dealers, just as other black tribes are classed as "Christians"; I have come across many of these Daggata, who are easily recognizable by the three, deep scars on their cheeks—a tribal mark. They are said by the other Soudan tribes to be cannibals, and are generally despised on this account and on account of the general belief in their being Jews. As far as I could discover in conversation with such of them as I have met in slavery, and who had learned Arabic, they are pagans, but adopt Mahomedanism very readily.

Mr. Haliburton again calls attention to Hanno's troglodytes. A large city of these strange cave dwellings I visited at Aïn Tarsil, in the Atlas Mountains, in 1887, and a somewhat full description written by myself was published in *The Times* of September 22 of that year. I quite agree with Mr. Haliburton that these caves were the work of the dwarfs,

the low ceilings, seldom over 5ft. 2in. in height, alone going far to prove this theory. These caves are not limited, as
Mr. Haliburton seems to think, to Southern Morocco, but I
found themn to exist, but in less numbers, in the mountains
between Tetuan and Sheshouan, on the borders of the Riff
country, and again to the east of Wagan in the mountains,
and again between Fez and S'frou, in the lower mountains of
the Beni M'tir, to the west of the "plain" road. In another
portion of his paper Mr. Haliburton mentions the "haik"
bearing the "eye." Does he not mean the Berber "s'lham"
or "bernous" of black woven goat hair, with the "eye" in
red and slightly decorated? The writer had one which he
bought off the back of a Berber in the Atlas Mountans, for
they are not by any means confined to the dwarf tribes, but
are worn all through the Atlas Mountains. The theory that
this "eye is the origin of the "Cyclopes" is by no means far
fetched.

It is to be hoped that if any reader possesses any knowledge of these dwarf tribes he will take this opportunity of
putting it before the world, for with a collection of notes
on the subject it would be far easier to follow up the study
of one of the most interesting and least known races of the
globe. With apologies for taking up so much of your valuable space,

Believe me, Sir, your humble and obedient servant,

Walter B. Harris

Dwarfs and Dwarf Worship

Letter to the Editor (*London Times*), September 17, 1891

J. E. Budgett Meakin

To the Editor of the *Times*.

Sir,—Contrary to my inclination, it has fallen to my lot
to refute the theory put forward by my friend Mr. Haliburton
at the Oriental Congress that a race of dwarfs exists between the Atlas and the Sahara. When preparing one of the
papers I read before the British Association, the secretary
of the section to which it belonged requested me to make
some statement regarding this subject, as it was believed to
have no foundation, and ought to be repudiated. I refused
to touch upon it unless it were brought up independently,
so it went uncontroverted. But in the third paper I read before the Oriental Congress, in view of the publication of
Mr. Haliburton's paper on "Dwarf Races," I felt bound to
express my opinion, lest I should seem by silence to con-
sent. My words were that the darker Berbers of the south
"are shorter and more thickly set than the mountaineers,
and, as a rule, more corpulent and 'jolly.' The reports published of a dwarf race occupying the district between the
Southern or Lesser Atlas and Guinea I place no credit in
whatever, believing them to be greatly exaggerated, and
distorted beyond recognition. I have never yet heard any

proof of their existence." I said this after having heard from Mr. Haliburton a few weeks ago the whole of his theory, with a rehearsal of his evidence, and after having, as the result of Mr. Haliburton's communications to me in Morocco some years ago, made special inquiries on the spot. Since the reading of my paper, I have been carefully through the evidence collected, with Mr. Haliburton, as I am as interested in the subject as he is, and would far rather that such a fascinating race should be discovered than not. The result has been a confirmation of my opinion that, whatever clues this evidence may afford, as proof it has no weight whatever.

Let me take, first, the most important documents, the letters of Europeans, all but one known personally to me, and whose statements are perfectly trustworthy. The sum of these is that individual dwarfs have been seen occasionally in Morocco, but very rarely. I can add my own testimony to that, as I have seen two or three in various parts of the country myself, but by no means so many proportionally as in England. My observations extend over a period of six years' uninterrupted residence and travel in Morocco, spent in amassing every kind of information regarding the country and its people, and, speaking Arabic. Yet I have never come across the slightest rumour of such a race, much as I should have liked to, and neither has one of Mr. Haliburton's witnesses except from himself; as their letters show. It is curious that the statement contained in the first letter from the witness unknown to me personally was pencilled by me in reply to Mr. Haliburton's inquiry, which had been handed to me for the purpose through a mutual friend. Thus my own evidence is twisted against me. In the discussion which followed my denial at the Oriental Congress, I explained that, though there might even be families of hereditary dwarfs in Akka, there could be no question as to the existence of a race or nation such as Mr. Haliburton believed in. If solitary specimens were sufficient proof of such, I could in 24 hours produce evidence of a secreted dwarf race in Camden-town, for several reliable witnesses had assured me that a number were occasionally seen there.

Then, as to native "depositions." As I have sat by Mr. Haliburton's side in Tangier and heard his cross-questioning, I know how much weight to attach to these. The questions, which mostly contained the answers, were seldom fully understood by the interpreter, being too excitedly spoken, and, very seldom reached the subject of examination, so the interpreter found it best, as a rule, to return stock answers such as "Yes, Sir," "Quite right," "Just so," &c., all of which provided abundant material for the most interesting notes. I could easily prove the existence of a race of giants anywhere in that fashion. I must make it clearly understood, however, that Mr. Haliburton is a man above suspicion of desiring to mislead, and I regret very much being obliged, in the interests of truth, to point out that, in his ignorance of the people and their language, he has been carried away by a will-o'-the-wisp.

There are two prominent points in his interesting theory. The first is that "one might live a hundred years in Morocco and never hear of these little folk," which is solemn fact; and the second is the accounting for this by the assertion that they are looked upon as so sacred that it would be a sin to mention them to Jews or Christians—a manifestly absurd idea. Any one with a knowledge of Orientals is aware that the most ridiculous fables exist among them as to the inhabitants of remote districts or those difficult of access. Would a collection of their remarkably corresponding descriptions of the genii (jinns) who are supposed to guard the treasure stored by "Christians" in the Atlas caves be any proof of their existence? In this nineteenth century we want something more sober by way of history than Münchausen, and by way of travel than Gulliver, or even, as a general description of the people, than "The Thousand and One Nights." The only two European travellers who have visited Akka, Rohlfs and De Foucauld (both living), were most curiously blinded by adverse fates when in that district, and perforce left all the glory of penetrating sight to Mr. Haliburton, who has never been nearer than the north coast of Morocco. Leo Africanus, whom I have proved to be the only reliable authority on the habits of these people, except De Foucauld, makes no mention whatever of such a race, though he descends to minutiæ regarding their neighbours. It is utterly absurd to imagine that the Moors could indulge in a superstitious dread of the discovery of these imaginary dwarfs, or that they could have so long maintained their secret.

Mr. Harris's letter in your issue of to-day throws no further light upon the subject, as his evidence goes no further than that of the others quoted. He is quite right about the Seedi Hamed or Moosa Brotherhood being composed of men from various parts of the country. I know many of them. They have nothing to do with the short people of the south beyond including many in their ranks, as their headquarters

is in that direction, in Soos. They are professional acrobats. The coincidence of the name Akka, that of a district
in Southern Morocco, with that of a district of dwarfs met
by Schweinfurth some two or three thousand miles distant,
is what probably at first led Mr. Haliburton astray. I pointed
out at the Congress that between these two points the Sahara
rolls, as effectual a barrier as the Mediterranean affords
between Europe and Africa. There is therefore no support
to be derived from this fact. Mr. Harris is quite right in
pointing out that Sidi Bárakah is a name only applied to
Moslem saints. There are many who bear this "title" of
normal proportions. It is a great mistake to suppose that
Mahomedans worship others than God. They plead with
saints innumerable to use their influence with the Deity,
that they may obtain what they desire, contrary to the popular idea as to their belief in an unchangeable decree. Mr.
Harris's explanation of the "Black Jews" coincides with
my own, though I have no doubt they are partly of Jewish
origin, and that there is much "Christian" blood among
many Berber tribes. The height of the Troglodyte caves in
the Atlas is the only proof that dwarfs ever lived there—if
the caves were ever used as dwellings. The cloak bearing
the "eye"—described in my paper on the Berbers and of
which I have two specimens here—is not a *haik* (blanket),
but a *khaneef*, or *khaidoos*, called in Algeria a *burnous*. It
is only worn by one section of the Berbers, in the Great
Atlas, as far as I know, and it was thence I brought mine.

If any one has actual proof of Mr. Haliburton's theory,
I shall be delighted to examine and recognize it, but till
then it should not be put forward as fact for the foundation

of other theories innumerable. I have already written to various parts of Morocco for independent inquiries to be made.

I am, Sir, yours respectfully,

Jas. Ed. Budgett Meakin, for some years Acting Editor of the *Times of Morocco*.

269, Camden-road, N., Sept. 14.

Dwarfs and Dwarf Worship

Letter to the Editor (*London Times*), September 21, 1891

R. G. Haliburton

To the Editor of the *Times*.

Sir,—It is satisfactory to know that Mr. Harris has returned safe and sound, after his wanderings among the tribes of the Atlas, and it is to be hoped that he will soon give us an account of his travels and their fruits. When I saw him in November last he promised to collect some of the ancient legends and traditions which are preserved by the tribes south of Mount Atlas, who are in many respects quite distinct from the northern Moors and it is probable that he has brought back a store of Susi and Draoui folklore. His inquiries into the gibberish or Oghama-like secret modes of speech of the Dra no doubt have led to interesting results. He also promised to look into the subject of the existence of a dwarf race, and his letter shows that he has been as good as his word. He is the fifth person who has made investigations into the subject, for I am only one of five. The subject was first taken up by myself in February, 1888, and was followed up last winter and spring. In the summer of 1888 Sir John Drummond Hay in Tangier, and Miss Day at the Tlemçen mission to the Berbers, very kindly hunted up some Dra or Susi people who had seen these dwarfs; and last winter, as there was a dwarf living at Fez, I wrote to Miss Herdman, of the Fez mission (a lady of whose abilities and knowledge of the Moors Mr. Harris and others had spoken most highly), asking her to make careful inquiries as to whether there was really a dwarf there, and whether a tribe of such dwarfs was known to exist south of Mount Atlas. Professor Flower had suggested my getting a showman to bring one of these dwarfs to England, so I went to a retired leader of a Sidi Hamed O Moussa troupe, living at Tangier, and urged him to go into the speculation. He evidently was taken aback when I spoke of the dwarf at Fez, and said that he himself had never heard of such a race, but that he would write to the dwarf in question about the matter. I knew at once what that meant, that he would forbid the dwarf from being seen by Christians, and I wrote to Miss Herdman that she would probably not be able to see him.

The following letter from her will show that I had gone to the very wrong man, as these dwarfs were ancestral. kinsmen of his tribe. Before a week had passed the poor dwarf was at the point of death.

"Fez, Feb. 4, 1891.

"Dear Mr. Haliburton,—There is a tribe of dwarfs inhabiting a part of Sus, called Oulad Sidi Hamed O Moussa, or Sidi Hamed Ben Moussa. Some of them are acrobats and come occasionally to Fez. They are expected in the spring. As the Court is at Morocco, I think they are more likely to go there, as there is more money going there. There is a man living at

Fez of the tribe. I know persons who know him. Unfortunately he is too ill to leave his bed at present. I am told he is likely to die, having been ailing a long time. They are about 4ft. high. Various persons from Sus have described them to me, and say that a woman is the size of an ordinary little girl, and a man with a beard is like a little boy. They are never called Akkas, or any name except that I have mentioned. Some are larger than others. Write to Morocco city, as they will he almost certain to be there for the festivities of the wedding of the Emperor's son.

"You may rely on the information I have given you, as I have it from various sources. There are no dwarfs between Fez and Morocco, as far as I know. With best regards, and ready to investigate anything in the interest of science and truth,

"I remain faithfully yours,

"Emma Herdman.

"P.S.—Our servant, a well-read Moor, did his best to bring correct news.

"The dwarfs are said to be rather dreaded, as they are expert thieves, for they climb on each other's shoulders, and so scale high walls. Others say they can climb like cats with no foothold."

That there is a tribe of these acrobats (who may perhaps sometimes get recruits from neighbouring tribes) will be seen not only by Miss Herdman's letter, but also by the statement of one of them, who had quarrelled with and disowned his tribe. The fact that one of these dwarfs was sent hundreds of miles to him to endeavour to reconcile him to his kinsmen shows that the Patiki have a religions or sacerdotal influence over their kindred acrobats.

"The name of the dwarf that died at Mogador eight or ten years ago was Hadfi Brahim Adusal" (a Mogador Jew called him Sidi Absolom Baraker). "Have seen many small people at Wadnoon, Adusal is their name. Hazora also is a name for them. You cannot tell one from the other. Some of the little people perform with the Sidi Hamed O Moussa. One of them was sent to reconcile me to my tribe, but did not succeed."

A native of Akka, belonging to the tribe Ait Psech, does not give a very flattering account of these dwarfs. Speaking of an ancient building at Ta-Punt, he says there are small figures in it, "some 18in., some 3ft. high; very odd looking; no man can understand them. They are called Patiki, and so are the little men. The little men are very ugly, and have no eyebrows, and have smooth faces. People are afraid of them."

I am told that at Tazzawalt, in the south of Sus, the chief of the acrobats, who is a saint and reigns as king, has always about him eight or ten of his ancestors, the dwarfs.

There has been some question raised as to the Bani Mountains. They are a low range of hills near the Sahara, extending from the Atlantic to near Tafilelt. It is also known as "the Mountain of the Christians." The subject is an interesting one, but I cannot trespass on your space by referring to it at greater length.

The distinctive name of the peculiar Cyclopean garment with the eye is Khanif.

I may add that, as there are so few of these dwarfs in northern cities, it is remarkable that eight Englishmen have seen one or more of them. One has seen three, two have seen two, and five have seen one. I did not expect at first that I should be able to get, in corroboration of the statements of natives, the positive testimony of any Europeans, as to their having actually seen and talked with these dwarfs.

I remain faithfully yours,

R. G. Haliburton.

Edwards's Hotel, Hanover-square, Sept. 16.

P.S.—Please allow me to add to yesterday's letter the following remarks as to Mr. Meakin's letter of the 14th, which appeared to-day.

On one point his memory must have deceived him. Before my last visit to Morocco in November last, I had not been there since 1887, and, in the interim, I spent six months in Algeria, where I got my first tidings of the existence of dwarfs south of Mount Atlas. When I went to Tangier last November Mr. Meakin had left that country. Therefore he must be under some mistake in his statement as to "having some years ago made special inquiries on the spot" "as the result of Mr. Haliburton's communications to me in Morocco." Nor did he sit beside me while I was examining natives. Even if he did so, the art of examining a witness is a matter of legal training and of long practice, and as Mr. Meakin, though an intelligent man, has had no legal training, and I am an old Q.C., and was cross-examining witnesses when he was spinning tops, I think he should omit this point from those on which he feels himself called upon to enlighten the public and myself.

Miss Day wrote from Tlemçen in Algeria to Tangier after my correspondence with her had closed; and there can be no doubt, therefore, that the pencil memorandum he made on a letter to her, must have been held sacred by her, and will never be "twisted" against himself.

Mr. Meakin says that my European informants do not state that there is a race of dwarfs, but they do not do so for a very good reason. They had never suspected that the dwarfs they had seen belonged to a. dwarf race, otherwise they would have at once published the fact, and, no doubt, as Mr. Meakin is engaged to give lectures on Morocco, they would not have escaped a long controversy with him.

There is only one more point which I shall refer to. Mr. Meakin says, "In the discussion which followed my denial at the Oriental Congress, I explained that, though there might even be families of hereditary dwarfs in Akka, there could be no question as to the existence of a race, or nation, such as Mr. Haliburton believes in." The three following extracts will suffice as an answer. The first is the statement of the acrobat, already quoted, "I have seen many small men at Wadnoon." He was examined by Mr. Broom, a native of Morocco, whose native language is Arabic.

An Ait Atta, previously examined, says that "there are dwarfs at Ahdeed in the Ait Messad (east of Demnat), about 1,500; and about 1,000 at Ait Messal; also at Ait Bensid, about 500." "The Ait Atta do not reverence the small people very much, though when we meet one, and do not know his name, we call him Sidi Baralker."

The son of the governor of a district in Akka gives the names of the three villages of dwarfs which are under his father's rule. Their number is about 400 in all.

A native of Tafilelt, speaking of a district farther east, says:— "The little people live near the river Dora, near Tinzone, in the Black Mountains, and trade with Tinzone. There are more than a thousand there."

I am informed that the dwarfs perished by hundreds in the great famine in 1879-82, and that their numbers were greatly reduced.

I may add that the passage quoted from Caillé is omitted in the English translation. He says of the dwarf who, he thought, reappeared at a station, though left behind at the last, "Ce petit homme, qui m'apparaisait comme un nain mystérieux."

September 17.

Some Further Notes on the Existence of Dwarf Tribes South of Mount Atlas

R. G. Haliburton

"With the precision of Herodotus before us ... we must admit that the little race of men seen by the Nasamonians exists to-day to the north of the Niger, but has not yet been discovered, or that it has disappeared from those regions."—Quatrefages, *Les Pygmées*, p. 25.

On the 2nd of September, 1891, a paper on "Dwarfs and Dwarf Worship," referring to some of the proofs that had come to light that there must be dwarf tribes in southern Morocco, was read by myself at a meeting of the Ninth Oriental Congress in London. In October-following a pamphlet embodying the paper read before the Congress, with statements of numerous informants (three of them dwarfs)[1] as to the localities in which they reside, their probable numbers, etc., was published by Mr. David Nutt, bookseller, London, and some months afterwards was specially reviewed in a paper by the President of the Khedivial Geographical Society, Cairo, H. E. Abbate Pacha.

A new light was subsequently thrown on the subject of dwarfs by Sir George Humphrey, Professor of Medicine in the University of Cambridge (see "British Medical Journal," Dec. 5, 1891). Dealing merely with European, *i.e.*, non-racial dwarfs, he divides them into two classes, "true dwarfs," who only differ from their race in size, and "dwarfs from rickets," who are stunted, and generally malformed and feeble. His statement that neither of these classes transmits its small size to the children, disposes of the theory that the dwarfs met with in Morocco are merely a few families of ordinary dwarfs. Far from being stunted and deformed through rickets, they are very strong, extremely courageous, and wonderfully active, and are, it is stated, feared by the other Moors. Nor can they be "true dwarfs," a class so rarely met with that though for more than half a century medical and other museums have been multiplied in France and England, those of the former country only possess one skeleton of a "true dwarf," while the only one to be seen in England is that presented to the Medical Museum at Cambridge by Sir George Humphrey himself in December, 1890. The chances of course of meeting with a "true dwarf" in a very sparsely populated country like Morocco would be infinitely more remote than among the many millions of inhabitants of France and Great Britain. If, then, a dozen dwarfs, not stunted or deformed by rickets, have found their way to northern Morocco, the inference is conclusive that they cannot be what Sir George calls "true dwarfs," but must be racial, and connected with some dwarf tribe.

But any doubt that might at first sight seem to exist on this point is settled when I mention that the dwarfs seen in Morocco are not diminutive Moors, resembling their countrymen in everything except size, but are so strikingly distinct from the other people of Morocco, that even if they were not dwarfs we should have to set them down as belonging to a different and peculiar race. Among the points which distinguish them from the Moors, Arabs, Berbers, Jews, Negroes, and Mulattoes of Morocco, are the following: their wonderful agility; a reddish complexion which is characteristic of almost all dwarf races, and which one of my informants describes as "like that of the Red Indians of America," or according to Schweinfurth in his account of the Akkas of the Albert Nyanza, "resembling the color of slightly roasted coffee"; and the peculiar woolly hair growing in tufts which generally distinguishes dwarf races and their offshoots.[2] They differ even in dress, etc., and shave their faces—an abomination to Moslem Moors. In all these particulars as well as in size they are precisely similar to the dwarfs of Equatorial Africa.

Should we meet in Europe with Mongolian-looking dwarfs, only about four feet high, with a yellow complexion, flat, broad faces, high cheek bones, and "pigtails," we should be disposed to suspect that a race of Chinese dwarfs must have found their way West, and that these peculiarities could not possibly be the result of ordinary European dwarfism.

So far at least as early ages are concerned, the idea is not a new one that dwarfs once existed south of Mount Atlas; for it has for some years been a subject of contention between French geographers and some French anthropologists. The former maintain that the place described by Herodotus where the Nasamonian explorers were captured by dwarf Troglodytes must have been an oasis in the north-western part of the Sahara, not far to the south or south-east of

Morocco. French geographers, the highest, if not the only, authorities on the ancient and modern geography of northern Africa, have for over half a century devoted much attention to the subject, and are therefore the best guides we can have as to the accounts given by Herodotus of the sandy region extending westwardly from the Nile to the Atlantic, and of the races that inhabited it. One of his descriptions[3] starts from Thebes, and includes what is now called the Libyan desert, the Sahara, and the Sahel, the term "the Pillars of Hercules" being used for "the Atlantic," or rather for "the farthest west."

The country of the Nasamonians, called by Procopius Zaba, is now known as the Oasis of Mzab. West of them were the Garamantes, now known as the Touaregs, who, he says, fought in four-horse chariots with the swift-footed Ethiopian Troglodytes. The cave-dwellers must have inhabited that rocky region, the southern flanks of the Atlas, which forms a barrier to the sands of the desert, and many of the spurs of which jut far out into the Sahara, and are sometimes called "the Saharan Atlas." These cave-dwellers no doubt belonged to the race of swift-footed Troglodytes seen by Hanno on the western coast of what is now called Morocco. The numerous chambers cut in the face of inaccessible cliffs in Morocco, and especially to the south of the Great Atlas, were probably made by these Troglodytes.

Another description[4] which Herodotus gives us of that region begins at Cyrene, or rather at Mzab, and tells us of "the sandy ridge" lying to the south of the wooded country inhabited by wild beasts, and extending westward to Cape Solois, now known as Cape Cantin, on the west coast of

Morocco. He, in fact, describes the present Timbuctoo caravan route from Tripoli to Dra. According to him, some young Nasamonian explorers went west for many days until they reached as oasis, where they were captured by a dwarf race of Troglodytes, who were all necromancers, and lived on a river which ran from west to east. Three large rivers, that rise near each other in Mount Atlas, run for a great distance in a south-easterly direction, the Ghir, the Zis and the Dra. Though the exact locality in question must remain a matter of conjecture, it must have been situated on one of these rivers, and must have been to the south or south-east of Morocco. It will be seen in "The Dwarfs of Mount Atlas" that several natives of that country describe a race of dwarf ostrich-hunters living in that part of the Sahara,[5] who are Marabouts, astrologers, magicians, and finders of hidden treasures, and who own a very small breed of remarkably swift ponies, and are called Teata Tajakants to distinguish them from the larger Tajakants living farther west, near Tinzint.

The dwarfs mentioned by Aristotle cannot have lived in Equatorial Africa, as they possessed a remarkably small breed of horses.

The rock-cut chambers in the Atlas, whether intended for storehouses or for residence or refuge, are so uniformly about five feet high that they most probably were made by dwarf Troglodytes.

Quatrefages says[6] that "with the precision of Herodotus before us, and the agreement which his narrative shows with material facts of a permanent nature, we must admit that the little race of men seen by the Nasamonians exists to-day to the north of the Niger, but has not yet been discovered, or that it has disappeared from those regions."

The views of French geographers on this point have been contested in an able article on the "Pygmies of Antiquity" in the last October number of *The Revue Historique* on the ground that we can find no trace of there ever having been dwarfs north of the Sahara.[7] By an odd coincidence a letter was received by me in that very month from Mr. Thomas Martin, now living at Crowborough, England, in which he said that, having become familiar with the peculiar klicks in vogue in the speech of South African tribes, who have inherited or borrowed them from the dwarf Bushmen, he was surprised in 1888 at hearing at Mogador, a port on the south-west coast of Morocco, some natives from Sus and the Sahara using klicks similar to those of South African races. He naturally came to the conclusion that the Bushmen must have in early ages found their way as far north as Mount Atlas.

The President, in the course of his paper on my pamphlet, drew attention to the peculiar indentation in dwarf skulls at the base of the nose. If this is confined to the skulls of African dwarfs, it would seem to indicate that it may possibly be connected with South African klicks, either as a cause or as an effect.[8] There cannot be a doubt that there is an extensive district to the south of Morocco, bounding southerly on the Sahara, which is called Akka, and is said to be the headquarters of the Atlas dwarfs; and also that there is another Akka on the shores of the Albert Nyanza, which is also inhabited by a dwarf race called Akka. Which was the original Akka? Quatrefages mentions a tradition among some dwarfs of Equatorial Africa, that the ancestors of their race came from the northwest, *i.e.*, from the direction of Morocco!

When Schweinfurth, and after him Miani, described the dwarfs of the Mombutto country, and were denounced as imposters, they had but little confirmatory evidence which they could rely on. As respects the question of the Atlas dwarfs, it is fortunate that sixty-five informants have testified to their having seen one or more of them, thirty-two (some of them dwarfs) having been able to describe dwarf tribes and villages south of the Atlas. Before a year elapses further definite information will, I hope, be obtained that will put an end to all question on this point. I may, meanwhile, mention that a few weeks ago I received from the Right Hon. Sir John H. Drummond Hay some notes in Shilhach (the Berber dialect, spoken generally south of the Atlas), written by a Sus Taleb of Saffi respecting the localities in Sus and the Sahara where ancient ruins are to be found. Of several of them the Taleb says, "These are places where the little people live. Their occupation consists in making mats from Esparto grass."

Footnotes

[1] See "Dwarfs of Mount Atlas " (David Nutt, London), 1891, pp. 14, 18, 24.

[2] I made no note of, as I did not credit, the statements of several natives of Morocco, that the bodies of the dwarfs are covered with hair, a peculiarity which I have since found is a characteristic of the dwarfs both of Central Africa and of Keltic tradition.

[3] B. IV., ch. 181, 170, 43, 44; B. II., ch. 31, and 32.

[4] B. II., ch. 31.

[5] According to Herodotus, Sataspes, while sailing south from the Pillars of Hercules, saw a "nation of little men."

[6] *Les Pygmées*, p. 25.

[7] The learned writer of that article, M. Paul Monceaux, on the 9th June, 1892, wrote to Mr. David MacRitchie as follows: "La brochure de votre ami, Mr. Haliburton, est une contribution trés curieuse et trés neuve a la question des Pygmées. ... Aprés avoir pris connaissance des faits precis et des temoignes dans "The Dwarfs of Mount Atlas" il me parait difficile de contester les conclusions de l'auteur; et je ne doute pas qu'un jour une nouvelle exploration methodique du Maroc ne vienne les confirmer."

[8] A resident for some years in the Andaman Islands says the natives have neither this indentation, nor klicks in their speech; and that they shave their faces and heads with sharp-edged shells. It is worthy of note that the names of their tribes are prefaced with *a-ka*. Why was the Sphinx (so venerably ancient a monument that it seems to connect the present with the dawn of Creation—the era of the dwarf god, Ptah, the Creator, and of the "first-created," half-animals, half-men) called "Akka"? Some of my South Morocco informants say that in the Dra Valley the name Pataïki (=fathers of our fathers, or ancestors) is applied both to dwarfs and to little monstrous images, part animal, part man. May not Akka, like "Pataïki," have once been applied to both?

Survivals of Prehistoric Races in Mount Atlas and the Pyrenees

R. G. Haliburton

In July last, while visiting the Parliamentary Library at Ottawa, Canada, and casually looking over the numbers of *Kosmos* for 1887, I was surprised at meeting with the following paragraph, headed *Les Pygmées de la Vallée de Ribas*, (New Series, vol. VIII, p. 59): "Professor Miguel Maratza has discovered in the valley of Ribas (province of Gerona, Spain) a community of very curious people whom the country people call *Nanos*" (Dwarfs?). "Their height does not exceed 1 m. 10, to 1 m. 15. These Pygmies are well built, and have a robust appearance. Their hair is red. Their face forms a perfect square. Their cheekbones are prominent, their jaw heavy, their nose flat, and their eyes, which are slightly oblique, resemble those of the Mongols. They have only a few scattered hairs on their face."

I could not find any further reference to the subject either in *Kosmos*, or in such other scientific periodicals as I was able to consult; but, as Stanley had not then told the world about his Congo dwarfs, and the subject of pygmy race had not attracted the large amount of public attention which it since has, it is probable that the paragraph in question escaped notice and has since been forgotten. It could not have been suggested by my having got tidings of the existence of dwarfs South of Mount Atlas, for my Insi servant first told me of the dwarfs who lived in Akka, the country adjoining his own, in January or February 1888. His statements and some confirmations that had so far come to light, were communicated in Sept. 1888 to the Geographical Section of the British Association, but without any expression of opinion on my part.

It is extremely interesting to note that *Ribas*, the home of the dwarfs of the Pyrenees, is the name of a place connected with a dwarf tribe in central Africa. In an article in the *Popular Science Monthly* (vol. XXXVI, p. 664, 1890) we are told that "on the shores of the Liba is another people called Kenkob, only three or four feet high." Another man gave Dr. Koelle a very similar account of a tribe called *Betsan*, living on the River *Riba*, evidently the same as *Liba*.

The announcement of the survival of a dwarf race in the Eastern Pyrenees has during the present summer been followed by another as respects a larger prehistoric race in the Eastern recesses of those little known and to a large extent unexplored mountains.

In the *Popular Science Monthly*, for May last, p. 39, in an article entitled "Cave dwellings of Men," we are told that at a recent meeting of the Royal Geograph. Society of Madrid, Dr. Bride gave an account of his exploration in a wild district in the province of Cáceres, which he represented as inhabited by a strange people who speak a curious patois and live in caves, and inaccessible retreats. They have a hairy skin, and have hitherto exhibited a strong aversion to mixing with their Spanish and Portuguese neighbours.

Roads have been recently pushed into the district inhabited by these *Jourdes*, and they are be ginning to learn the Castilian language, and to attend the fairs and markets.

This announcement was not altogether unexpected by me from my having met ten years ago, in Berthelot's *Antiquities Canariennes* (1880), a full account of a similar discovery, made about the end of the 15th Century, of a community of harmless savages in a secluded district in Spain, whose only religious rites consisted in their offering fruits and flowers to their Deity on the tops of mountains. As they were not true believers, and were not likely to become such, as they could not speak in an intelligible language, the only thing that could be done with them was to burn them. It is not unlikely, as Berthelot suggests, that they were survivals of a primitive Berber race, such as peopled the Canary Islands, and North Africa; and we are reminded that in their offerings of fruits and flowers they resembled the Guanches, and also the primitive races of the West Indies, and the simple Toltecs of Mexico, the followers of the divine apostle of peace, Quetzalcoatl.

What is the language spoken by these *Jourdes*? Is it connected with Berber, or with Keltic, or with Basque? The problem can easily be solved, and I trust will be cleared up at the proposed Congress at Lisbon on the 20 Sept. In July last through Dr. Leitner I drew the attention of the Organizing Committee at Lisbon to the great importance of at once communicating with Professor Maratza and Dr. Bride, respecting their discoveries in the Eastern and the Western Pyrenees; it was urged that they should be invited to attend, and to bring with them, if possible, one or more of the

Jourdes and Nains. If these suggestions can be carried out, no doubt most interesting and important results will follow. It is difficult on an Ethnological point of view to exaggerate the importance of the discoveries of Professor Maratza and Professor Bride, for if they can be substantiated, (as we have every reason to expect), they will supply a connecting link between the prehistoric cavedwellers, the brownies, and the "nocanny" dwarfsmiths of European folklore and fairy tales with similar races now existing from mount Atlas to the Kalahari desert of South Africa.

The well known red cap of Morocco, called *Fez*, from the city where it is principally made, and a form of which is worn by the Portuguese, and especially by the people of the Azores, is of no little interest, as it is used by the dwarf Laplanders, and was worn by the dwarfs of Keltic and Teutonic tradition, who are therefore known to folklore as *Red Caps*.

It is hoped that before the end of the year a very competent explorer will have reached the secluded homes of the Atlas dwarfs; but it is likely that even more important discoveries will have been previously made in the Pyrenees, that will be a warning to the large class that, being overburthened with a little knowledge, know every thing that is worth knowing, and therefore look on anything outside their range as an imposture or a delusion. Thanks to such people, Schweinfurth and Miani, when they announced the existence of their dwarf Akkas, were set down as Munchausens. As the Greater part of the vast unknown country South of Mount Atlas has never been visited by a European, those who scouted the idea that there could be there tribes of dwarfs hitherto unknown, will be effectually silenced should the *Jourdes* and the *Nains* prove to be now in existence within easy reach of health seekers and Cook's tourists.

Dwarfs and Dwarf Worship

Letter to the Editor (*Nature*), January 21, 1892

Harold Crichton-Browne

In the slow course of post in this Protectorate I have just received copies of the *Times* of September 3 containing Mr. R. G. Halliburton's (*sic*) paper on "Dwarf Races and Dwarf Worship," and of September 14 and 22, containing subsequent correspondence on the same subject. Having crossed the Atlas Mountains at several different points, and approached the district which is indicated by Mr. Halliburton as the original home and hidden sanctuary of his diminutive and venerated people, I have read his paper with much interest and may perhaps be permitted to criticize his conclusions. My chief during my expedition to Morocco, that distinguished traveller Mr. Joseph Thomson, is, I believe, at present in Katanga, and therefore more inaccessible than I am; but when he is able to speak on the subject, his judgment on the case which Mr. Halliburton has very elaborately set up will not, I am confident, be different from mine.

Mr. Halliburton begins with a statement that is at once startling and decisive. The information he has collected puts it, he says, beyond question that there exists in the Atlas Mountains, only a few hundred miles from the Mediterranean, a race of dwarfs only 4 feet high, who are regarded with superstitious reverence or are actually worshipped, and whose existence has been kept a profound secret for 3000 years. Such an emphatic assertion ought to rest on clear and irrefragable evidence; and I read Mr. Halliburton's paper in constant expectation of the proofs of his remarkable discovery, but reached the end of it without coming on a shred of testimony in support of his contention, of the slightest value to anyone acquainted with Morocco and the Moors. The paper is highly discursive, and abounds in what seem to me far-fetched and irrelevant speculations, on the connection between ancient Moorish poems and Greek mythology, on the derivation of the Phoenician deities, and on the meaning of Moorish habits and customs; but the only evidence, confirmatory of its thesis, adduced in it and in Mr. Halliburton's subsequent letters, amounts to this: that six Europeans have seen dwarfs in Morocco; that an indefinite number of natives have romanced about dwarfs in their usual way; that there are in Morocco artificial caves—presumably dwellings—of such small size as to suggest that they must have had very short inhabitants; and that there have come down to us from antiquity traditions as to Troglodytes who dwelt in the Atlas Mountains.

Mr. Halliburton's European witnesses are unimpeachable; and had my friend Mr. Hunot, whose knowledge of the country is extensive and accurate, distinctly said that there is a race of dwarfs in Morocco, I should not have ventured to contradict him. But all that Mr. Hunot says, in the long paragraph quoted from his letter, is that he recollects an adult dwarf of about the height of a boy of ten or

eleven years of age who lived and died in Mogador. All
that Captain Rolleston says is that he saw in Tangiers a
dwarf of about thirty-five or forty years of age 3 to 4 feet
in height, and of an unusually light complexion. All that
Mr. Carleton says is that he has seen a dwarf at Alcazar.
All that Sir John Drummond Hay says is that he hunted up
at Tangiers some Sus and Dra people who had seen dwarfs.
All that Miss Day says is that she had done the same at
Telcmen. All that Mr. Harris says, of his own knowledge,
is that he has seen two dwarfs—one at Fez, about 4 feet 2
inches in height, and of a light brown colour; and the other,
about whom no particulars are given, somewhere in the
country. All that Miss Herdman, whom I had the pleasure
of meeting at Fez, says is that she has never seen a dwarf
in Morocco, but that she has heard of one, and has drawn
out tales about a tribe of dwarfs from her native servants.
All that Mr. Halliburton himself says to the point is that he
has seen and measured a very timid and obliging dwarf of
about thirty years of age, 4 feet 6 inches in height, and of a
peculiar reddish complexion, in Tangiers.

Let me add to Mr. Halliburton's list of European witnesses. I have myself seen two dwarfs in Morocco—one in
Fez, and the other in some northern town (I cannot for the
moment recollect which, and have of course no papers to
refer to). The first of these might perhaps have passed as a
true dwarf—a man of small size, but well proportioned, like
Tom Thumb; but the other was certainly a disease-dwarf,
with a large unshapely head and trunk, and little bowed
legs, like Canny Elshie, or the Wise Wight o' Mucklestane
Moor. Rickets are not unknown in Morocco. I have no doubt

that that malady is common in certain districts periodically visited by famine or devastated by war, and in which infant feeding is not conducted on scientific principles; and the probability is that men and women of stunted and distorted growth are more numerous in proportion to population in Morocco than they are in England. The wonder is to me that the number of instances of the occurrence of dwarfs in Morocco, which Mr. Halliburton in his long-continued researches has been able to establish, is so exceedingly small; and that one dwarf, for example he of Fez, has, like a stage army, to do duty several times over. But had he succeeded in identifying ten times the number of dwarfs that he has actually traced out, he would only have proved that dwarfs exist in Morocco as in all other countries, and would not have advanced a step towards proving his proposition that there is a tribe of dwarfs in the Atlas. I know a little Scotch town in which there are three dwarfs; but it would be scarcely legitimate to infer from that fact that there is a concealed clan of MacManikins in the Grampians. That the dwarfish condition in the dwarfs described by Mr. Halliburton was an accidental variation, and not a racial characteristic, is rendered more than probable by the fact that two of them—the only two who are reported to have had families—had offspring of normal stature.

The native reports about dwarfs and dwarf tribes, which Mr. Halliburton sets forth in much detail, are obvious fictions—of the kind which the professional story-teller pours forth copiously every day in the Soko in scores of Moorish towns and villages, only adapted, of course, to the requirements of an eager English listener. The names of the reporters are

not given, nor are the opportunities they possessed of ob-
taining the information they convey explained; while some
of the practices they attribute to the dwarfs—such as finding of treasure by writing on wood, and the feeding of
horses on dates and camels' milk with the view of render-
ing them swift of pace—I have heard ascribed to tribes in
the Atlas that are certainly not composed of dwarfs.

Morocco is the hot-bed of fable, and infested by the
cock-and-bull, and I can picture to myself the grave delight
with which the natives questioned by Mr. Halliburton would
stimulate his curiosity and then satisfy it. Mr. Halliburton
emphasizes the fact that he is a Q.C., and accustomed to
cross-examination; but British perjury and Moorish men-
dacity have little in common, and are to be fathomed by
entirely different methods. The way in which he measured
the Tangiers dwarf, Jackin (he actually took 2 inches off
his height because a native who was present told him that
Jackin had raised his heels to that extent while being measured), casts some doubt on his powers of observation;
while the extracts from his diary show that no process of
sifting has been carried out, but that everything favourable
to his theory has been thankfully received. I would undertake to collect in Morocco in a month's time native testimony in support of the existence of a tribe of giants in the
Atlas, or of a tribe of men with six digits on each hand,
quite as specious and convincing as that which Mr. Halliburton has accumulated in favour of the existence of a tribe
of dwarfs. Even if the natives interrogated by Mr. Halliburton had no wish to deceive or to please him, much would
depend on the intelligence and honesty of his interpreter,

and on the exact terms employed. Only those who have tried can realize how difficult it is to get precise information on any subject out of natives of Morocco.

If the caves in Morocco are to be regarded as at one time the dwellings of dwarfs, then it is clear that dwarfs must at one time have been in complete possession of the country, for such caves are to be found all over it. The most remarkable of them which I have visited at Tassimet, about two days' journey from Demnat—caves which Europeans had never before explored, and which were excavated in a rock by the side of a waterfall—were in many instances too small even for the accommodation of dwarfs; and as they yielded to our digging fragments of bone and of pottery, it seemed probable that they had been places of sepulture and not of habitation. Such caves have also undoubtedly been used sometimes for the storage of grain, like the underground metamors; and the invariable answer returned to our inquiries about their origin was that they had been made by the *Romi,* or Christians. Never on any occasion did I hear them ascribed to dwarfs.

The classical tradition that there were dwarfs in the Atlas is unworthy of serious consideration in the absence of any observation suggesting that it had other than an imaginative foundation. "Nearly all the myths of Greece," says Mr. Halliburton, "are laid in Mount Atlas," and monsters more extraordinary than dwarfs must have dwelt there if these myths are to be received as of historical authority.

I have tried to prove that the evidence given in favour of the existence of a tribe of dwarfs in the Atlas is utterly trivial and untrustworthy; and I shall now endeavour to show that the evidence that can be called to discredit that hypothesis is cogent and convincing. The dwarfs are described by Mr. Halliburton as brave, active, agile, swift-footed, as possessing a vigorous breed of ponies, as experts in the pursuit of the ostrich, and as trading in the Sahara and at Tassamalt. Is it to be believed that being all this, and being very numerous—there are, Mr. Halliburton says, about 1500 of them in Ait Messad, about 1500 at Akdeed, about 1000 at Ait Messal, about 500 at Ait Bensid, and about 400 in three Akka villages—is it to be believed, I ask, that these swarming and enterprising dwarfs would have allowed themselves to be bottled up in a cleft in the Atlas Mountains, so that only half-a-dozen specimens of them have found their way to the great towns to the north of the Atlas, where are to be found numerous representatives of all the other Atlas tribes? Is it to be believed again, that the existence of such a peculiar and notorious tribe, known, Mr. Halliburton tells us, to all Moors, should have been concealed from all the inquisitive travellers who have penetrated into the interior of Morocco, to be revealed to Mr. Halliburton standing at its outer gateway? Leo Africanus, whose account of Morocco is marvellously minute and accurate, and who enumerates its tribes, has not a word to say about dwarfs. De Foucauld, who visited Akka, is equally silent about them; and so is Rohlfs, who explored the valley of the Dra. Not one traveller in Morocco has ever heard even a rumour or dark hint relating to them.

Thomson and I spent some months in the Atlas in constant communication with natives of every class, and in all the strange legends, histories, and adventures narrated to us by the camp brazier, in the *fondak* or the *kasba*, there was never a distant reference to a Moorish Liliput; and be it remembered our servants knew that we had a keen eye and ear for curios, human and inhuman. In all our wanderings in the Atlas we never met a dwarf, and indeed, at a great gathering of people at which we were present, at the feast of Aid el Assir at Glawa we were much struck by the height of the men. Mr. Aissa, who is quoted by Mr. Halliburton as having seen one of the tribe of dwarfs east of Demnat, was our interpreter for three months, and conversed with us with the utmost freedom on all conceivable subjects, and he never adverted to this dwarf story. I have had several long talks with Mr. Hunot, whom Mr. Halliburton also quotes—conversations covering a wide range of topics, amongst them the origin of the caves already alluded to—and he certainly at that time had no belief that they had ever been tenanted by dwarfs, or that there was any dwarf tribe in the country. It is especially noteworthy that Du Bekr, the confidential agent of the British Government at the Court of Morocco, replied to Sir William Kirby Green that no Moor had ever heard of a race of dwarfs in the country. Sir William knew how to interrogate a Moor, and as he accepted Du Bekr's statement, I have no doubt that Du Bekr was speaking the truth.

Until the existence of a race of dwarfs in the Atlas Mountains is proved, it is idle to indulge in guesses at the reasons which have led to the fact of its existence being jealously kept secret; so I shall not follow Mr. Halliburton in the argument by which he seeks to show that the race has been regarded with superstitious reverence, and so kept

apart. In all countries, at all times, I believe dwarfs and
deformed persons have been looked at askance by the ignorant and superstitious. In Scotland they were regarded
as fairies of a brutal and malignant type; and in Morocco I
have no doubt they have been credited with the possession
of the evil eye and of other pernicious powers. But to maintain that a tribe of them has ever been held sacred and worshipped in the heart of a Mahometan country that is fiercely
fanatical is to do violence to our fundamental conceptions
of Islam.

Mr. Halliburton's statements about the origin and habits
of his supposed tribe of dwarfs are not more worthy of discussion than his theory of the causes which have led to their
concealment. They are derived from native sources of the
most tainted description, and are either pure inventions, or
concoctions of truth and falsehood. We are told that a tribe
of acrobats—the Ait Sidi Hamed O Moussa (the tribe of
the son of Moses)—is an offshoot of the Aglimien dwarfs,
living between the Dra and Akka; that they are a rather small
race with a light red complexion; and that dwarfs perform
with them in Southern Morocco, but avoid the coast towns
where Europeans are; and that they are smiths and tinkers.
Now, the paragraph setting forth these statements contains
just as much error and confusion as it is possible to cram
into so many words. The Sidi Hamed O Moussa are not a
tribe at all, but the followers of a saint whose Kuba is not
far from Taradant. Their troupes are made up of men drawn
from various parts of the country; and it would be as correct
to regard the Jesuits as a tribe, and describe their ethnic
characteristics, as it is to assign distinctive features to the

Sidi Hamed O Moussa. Then, as a matter of fact, they are not unusually small men, they are not smiths and tinkers, and they never have dwarfs performing with them either in town or country. I saw several troupes of them in Southern Morocco, and can testify that they are of average size and of the usual Moorish tint; that they follow a more profitable trade than that of tinkering; and that they have no dwarfs among them.

Mr. Halliburton strongly advises European travellers and tourists to abstain from any attempt to enter the districts of Morocco inhabited by the dwarfish race, as they would inevitably, while doing so, be murdered or robbed, whether Moslems, Jews, or Christians. The advice is judicious, for open-mouthed travellers of any persuasion, in quest of dwarfs, are not unlikely to be murdered or robbed in any part of Morocco except in those coast towns to which Mr. Halliburton has apparently confined his own wanderings in the country. European travellers of another sort, however—resolute, incredulous men, explorers, and pioneers of trade and commerce—will certainly before long penetrate all those regions where the dwarfish race has been located by Mr. Halliburton. Remembering what I have heard on good authority of the resources of some of those regions, and the indications I have seen of the mineral wealth of that region to the south of the Atlas where Mr. Halliburton has placed the original home of his dwarfs, I feel disposed to exclaim, like the old sailor in Millais's famous picture "The North-West Passage": "It can be done, and England ought to do it!" When, however, these regions are opened up, I feel sure that, amongst much that is wonderful in them, there will be found no tribe of dwarfs hemmed in by religious sentiment.

To those interested in the generation and growth of myths in modern times, and under Congress culture, Mr. Halliburton's dwarf-story cannot but afford an instructive study.

Harold Crichton-Browne
Macloustie Camp, Bechuanaland,
November 15, 1891

The "Dwarfs" of Mount Atlas

Letter to the Editor (*London Times*), January 10, 1893

Walter B. Harris

To the Editor of the *Times*.

Sir,—Although, perhaps, of no great importance either ethnologically or archæologically, the question as to whether a race or tribes of dwarfs existed on the Atlas range aroused last year some discussion in the English newspapers. Much contradictory evidence was given on both sides, and the question remained as uncertain, to those not absolutely taking part in the matter, after the conclusion of the correspondence, as it had previously been.

It may be remembered that the subject was started by the reading of a paper by Mr. R. G. Haliburton at the Congress of Orientalists in London. Mr. Haliburton stated that for some years he had made a special study of the question, and shortly after gave the results up to that date of his researches in a pamphlet entitled "The Dwarfs of Mount Atlas."

Were it not that I think I am able to throw a little further light upon what has already been stated I would not venture, Sir, to take up your valuable space by reopening the question.

I returned to Tangier but three days ago from a journey in Southern Morocco, in which I was accompanied by Mr.

R. G. Cunninghame-Graham. Hearing there, both from native sources and also from the members of the Scotch Mission, of rumours of small people inhabiting the upper ranges of the Atlas, Mr. Graham and I left Morocco city early in November for Amzmiz, a small town and bashalik at the foot of the Atlas Mountains. This was not the fast time I had visited this region, and the surrounding valleys were tolerably well known to me. Continuing our inquiries here we were successful in gaining all the information required, the Governor of the place himself informing us that a number of these little people were nominally under his jurisdiction, but, as a matter of fact, did not acknowledge the Moorish Government or pay taxes. On making further inquiries we discovered that one of the Governor's own soldiers was a dwarf from these regions. The soldier in question was easily found; in fact, he presented himself before even we commenced to look for him. In height he was slightly over 4ft., certainly under 4ft. 6in., of reddish brown colour, smooth face, except for a few hairs on the chin, and dressed in the ordinary costume of a Government cavalry soldier. He was a native of the snowy peaks of the Atlas above Imintella, one of the places Mr. Haliburton mentions in his pamphlet as being inhabited by these tribes. The following day we visited Imintella, without, of course, coming across any dwarfs. However, the existence of a dwarf people was far from being proved by the fact that we had met face to face a single specimen of a dwarf, or the fact that he, in common with the Governor and inhabitants of Amzmiz, assured us of their existence. Continuing our journey through the provinces of Mzuda and Mjat we entered the bashalik of Dueran. Here unexpectedly we were once more brought face to face with members of these small tribes, meeting a caravan of donkeys driven by seven men, none of whom were certainly above 4ft. 6in. in height. They were of various ages, one almost a boy, the others older. One wore a thick gray beard and one a small black beard. They seemed more surprised and amused to see us than we to see them, but as they spoke only Shlehah I was not able to communicate with them, they not comprehending any Arabic, nor did they understand the Shlehah of my Sus man. I think it is needless to mention the further cases we met with. In all we saw, perhaps, 13 or 14 of these dwarfs, nor did we meet with one single negative to the question I repeatedly asked as to their existence. It may be said that the fact that even 14 dwarfs were met with does not go to prove the existence of a tribe or tribes, yet the fact that a true dwarf is rare all the world over, the circumstance of meeting with such a considerable number is convincing.

Although, perhaps, our visit to the Atlas may tend to prove the existence of small people, it will certainly have a damping effect upon the many romances woven up with their existence. In the first place it was stated that these dwarfs were not Moslims. Such is not the case; not only are they followers of the prophet Mahomed, but they are the most strict observers of their religion. Again, the fact was stated that the reason why the Moors were so reticent in mentioning these people was that they were considered holy. Such, again, is apparently far from the truth. The fact of the matter is that so far from being holy they are looked upon as the very opposite, not from any superstition, but because, inhabiting the upper ranges of mountains which, for the greater part of the year, are covered in snow, at war with all men, inaccessible in their fastnesses, they hold at bay any overtures of the Moors to bring them under the sway of the Sultan. They are described as a wild people, living in built houses in the rocks and snow, hunting mouflon with extraordinary agility, and. given to shooting any one penetrating into their domains; and this description I believe to be true. Another reason of the fact that their existence is not spoken of by Moors is that in the Atlas Mountains their neighbours consider them as nothing extraordinary, and more particularly because, being independent, they are unable to descend the northern slopes of the Atlas to buy grain, &c., as they are imprisoned by their nominal Governors whenever caught. Those we were fortunate enough to see were in a district where the Governor had been killed, and where, for the time being at least, there was no forcible representative of the Moorish Government. Having thus nothing to fear they had descended to the lower slopes of the Atlas to do their marketing, as a nearer and more convenient spot than the southern slopes, to which they usually resort, as, being further removed from any seat of Government, they are able to frequent these southern slopes without fear of falling into the power of the local Kaids.

Mr. Haliburton goes further. He speaks of large tribes of "pygmies" living to the east of Wad Draa. Of these I am not able to speak, as such evidence as I was able to obtain was so contradictory as to allow of no fair estimate being given of its value. Perhaps Mr. Haliburton may be right that pygmies do exist there, but I think that it is now conclusively proved that the small people of Mount Atlas are not "pygmies"—that they are, in fact, merely a certain collection of Shleh tribes, who, through the high altitudes at which they live, and the extremes of climate they are subject to, from their poverty and inability to grow crops, from the scarcity and bad quality of such food as they are able to collect, have, in the lapse of centuries, become of almost extraordinarily stunted growth. Why then have they not been seen by former travellers? The answer is simple. Both Sir Joseph Hooker and Mr. Joseph Thomson, almost the only Europeans who have ever visited the Atlas, were during their travels entirely in lands governed by Kaids representing the Sultan, and the very proximity of these Kaids would drive the "small people" to a distance, who would never on any account visit their castles. It is for this reason alone that the existence of a stunted race of Shleh people must have failed to have attracted their notice. Yet it must not be thought that it is only the so-called dwarfs who set the Sultan's authority at naught. There are also many tribes of ordinarily-sized men who are independent; but inhabiting the most rigorous, inaccessible, and lofty parts of the whole range—the reason I believe of their small stature—the "dwarfs" have failed to attract, from their poverty and the barren nature of their country, that greed and avarice which is the sole cause of Mulai el Hassan's war expeditions.

Returning *via* Mtuga to Mogador we visited *en route* the caves of Ain Tarsilt, described by myself in *The Times* of September 23, 1887. All that need be repeated here is that the caves show very considerable skill and labour in their excavation by the troglodytes, and the fact that in none of the caves I entered are the roofs above 5ft. from the floor proves almost conclusively, taking into account the amount of labour spent on the walls, windows, doors, &c., the fact that the inbabitants must have been dwarfs.

Whether it is the descendants of these dwarfs whom Mr. Haliburton believes to be living on the Wad Draa I am unable even to venture an opinion, nor can I consider the information I was able to collect regarding a vast original civilization in that district sufficiently confirmatory or negative to be worth putting forward here.

If pygmies inhabited the caves of Ain Tarsilt, and not only the lowness of the roofs, but alcoves under five feet in length in the walls, doubtless forming beds, lead us to believe that such was the case, it may yet be proved that Mr. Haliburton's pygmy tribes are not the myths they have been stated to be, but live realities.

It may be possible that the dwarfs that Mr. Graham and myself saw are the remnants of the troglodytes, driven from their former abodes, who have taken refuge in the most accessible portions of the Atlas range as a protection against their enemies; but, tempting as this theory is, I find myself forced to believe that they owe their small stature to the climatic influences and the rigorous conditions of life in the country they inhabit. Having now clearly shown that tribes of abnormally small stature inhabit the upper peaks of the Atlas, there yet remains to be proved the question of the pygmies of Wad Draa, and many most interesting subjects pertaining to their existence. The fact that Mr. Haliburton's statement of the existence of a small race on the Atlas Mountains met at the time with much denial and a considerable amount of scoffing, and has now been shown to be true, renders it not improbable that in time the rest of his researches into the question of Southern Morocco may equally be confirmed.

Apologizing, Sir, for occupying so much of your valuable space, believe me your obedient servant,

Walter B. Harris.

Tangier, Dec. 31, 1892.

Mr. Haliburton's Dwarfs

Letter to the Editor (*The Academy*), July 22, 1893

J. S. Stuart-Glennie

I happen only to have just seen the Academy of July 8, with the letter by Mr. Haliburton on the "Holy Land of Punt," in which he refers to his paper in the *Asiatic Quarterly* on "Racial Dwarfs in the Atlas and the Pyrenees."

But the result of my correspondence, when lately in the South of France, with all the British Consuls and French savants likely to be specially acquainted with the ethnology of the Pyrenees, so completely negatived Mr. Haliburton's assertions, that I did not think it worth while to undertake the journey which I had proposed in order to see for myself these dwarfs of Mr. Haliburton's. And surely, before the reiteration of his assertions on this subject, Mr. Haliburton ought himself, if not to have explored the Pyrenees, at least to have entered into communication with the French savants to whom I have alluded, and particularly with M. Cartailhac, director of L'Anthropologie, who resides at Toulouse, within half a day's journey of the Pyrenean valleys in which Mr. Haliburton locates his dwarfs.

No less interesting than the discovery of dwarfs is the Pyrenees would be the discovery of dwarfs in the Atlas. But one cannot but fear that any attempt seriously to verify

Mr. Haliburton's assertions about the Atlas, which he has never, I believe, even approached, and particularly about the Holy Land of the Egyptians "at the head of the Dra Valley, with its most convenient access to the sea at Massa, opposite the Canary Islands," may have such a result as had my attempt to verify his assertions about the Pyrenees. "Racial Dwarfs?" "No!" But "certains goitreus de petite taille, sans doute."

J. S. Stuart-Glennie

Athenaeum Club: July 16,1893

Racial Dwarfs in the Pyrenees
Letter to the Editor (*Nature*), July 27, 1893

J. S. Stuart-Glennie

Being on the Riviera when I received *Nature* of January
26 with Mr. Haliburton's letter on the above subject, I proposed to act on his suggestion, and, on my way back to
England, to explore the region indicated. To ensure, however,
that the proposed exploration should not be a wild-goose
chase, I first entered into communication with all the British
consuls and French savants likely to have special knowledge
of the subject, and more particularly with M. Cartailhac,
director of l'Anthropologie, and who resides at Toulouse,
within little more than a half-day's journey from the valleys
named by Mr. Haliburton. I was favoured with interesting
replies from all those to whom I had written with the single
exception, very curiously, of our consul at Barcelona, a
letter from whom you published, and who appears to have
been Mr. Haliburton's chief authority. As to the replies I
received, I need only say that they so strongly negatived
the assertion of there being "racial dwarfs," though admitting that there are "certains goitreux de petite taille," in the
Pyrenean valleys, that I did not think it worth while to make
the proposed journey. And as Mr. Haliburton repeats, in
the current *Asiatic Quarterly*, the assertions made in *Nature*,

I feel bound to state these facts, though I may say that I quite agree with him as to the probability of a former wide distribution of dwarf races, and should have found Pyrenean dwarfs, had they been discoverable, in most interesting relations to the Ligurian giants, whose caves I had been exploring at Baoussé Roussé—the "Red Rocks" of Grimaldi.

J. S. Stuart-Glennie
Athenæum Club, July 10

Racial Dwarfs in the Atlas and the Pyrenees

R. G. Haliburton

In my "Dwarfs of Mount Atlas" (David Nutt, October, 1891), a second letter from Mr. Walter B. Harris appeared, who stated that early in November he would visit Morocco, and clear up the subject. Had he carried out his intention, it is now plain that he would have put an end to all discussion on the question before the end of December, 1891; but when the time for his leaving for Morocco had arrived, he was on his way to Yemen as "special correspondent of the *Times*," where he wrote some very interesting letters as to that unknown country.

A year later, members of the Scotch Mission to Southern Morocco discovered that there were, beyond question, in the Great Atlas, and almost in sight of that city, *tribes* of dwarfs such as I had described; and one of the Mission subsequently gave an account in the *Times of Morocco* of pygmies that had been seen, men and women, bathing together in the sacred waters at the tomb of Mulai Ibrahim.

Mr. Harris, who accompanied Mr. Cunninghame Graham on a round trip through Northern Morocco, heard from the Scotch Mission that there were dwarf tribes in the Atlas, a statement which the Moors fully confirmed; and he subsequently met with fourteen of these dwarfs at Amzmiz, and other places, height 4 ft. to 4 ft. 6 in., with a reddish-brown complexion.

There is now no question raised by anyone as to the existence of dwarf tribes in the Atlas; but the *Times of Morocco*, in admitting the fact, tried to account for it by a theory which no anthropologist will accept, namely that these dwarfs are stunted descendants of big rebel Berbers, who, driven by tax-collectors to inaccessible mountain ranges, had become dwarfed by cold and hard living. No instance of mountaineers being dwarfed by cold into pygmies, smaller than Andaman Islanders, is known to science; and as the southern slopes of the Atlas and the secluded country below offered a safe home and refuge to these people, they must have lived in the Atlas voluntarily. Mr. Silva, an engineer formerly in the employ of the Moorish Government, several years ago discovered in some high ranges of the Great Atlas an independent and warlike race of Jews, who, so far from being stunted, were much larger and more robust than other Barbary Jews.

While the fact of there being dwarf tribes in the Atlas was being conclusively established, a similar discovery was made of the existence of precisely similar racial dwarfs in the Pyrenees and other parts of Spain. Mr. Macpherson, our consul at Barcelona, at my request, caused careful enquiries to be made in the Eastern Pyrenees, the results of which he stated were conclusive as to there being racial dwarfs there, principally in the Val de Ribas, 1 metre to 1 m. 17 c. in height, copper-coloured, with flat broad noses and red hair, active and robust.

Some years ago a writer in *Kosmos* described them in similar terms, and spoke of their hair as woolly, and their eyes as slightly Mongolian-looking.

An Austrian merchant has informed me that he saw in the market-place in Salamanca similar dwarfs.

My attention was attracted last winter by an old Murcian peasant-woman, who had very decided *"dwarf klicks,"* similar to those that are in use in South Africa and Southern Morocco, and I suspected that she must have got the habit of "eating words" from dwarf ancestors. On inquiry I found that I was right; she said that these klicks came to her from some *"Nano"* or "dwarf" ancestors. In four out of six generations a "nano" had appeared. Her daughter and grand-daughter were under three feet eleven inches in height. In other half-breed Nano families dwarfs sometimes appear that look in every respect like African dwarfs.

We find in the Palæolithic and Neolithic ages traces of two dwarf races; those of the first era of an inferior type with a head projecting behind, and with oddly-curved thigh-bones, the joints of which, according to Huxley's acute conjecture, must have caused these *Neanderthal* or *Iberian* dwarfs to turn their toes in and to waddle in their walk. A very similar type is now found in parts of Central Africa, who are inferior to the Akka dwarfs, and who walk in the way mentioned. The dwarf on the monuments described by Wilkinson is one of them evidently, as he has a head projecting behind, in a singular way, and a flat forehead, probably the result of artificial flattening, such as is seen among American Indians. The Egyptian artist has also tried to give a full face portrait showing how the dwarf turned in his toes in walking.

The old Murcian half-breed Nano woman says that there are also two species of Nanos in Spain; one, a bad lot, of a low type, who are *Gitanonanos*, and live in caves and who are called Tartari, and walk in a ludicrous way, with toes turned in.

The other, who are better-looking, are *Castillano-Nanos*, who came to Spain originally from an ancient city beyond Morocco, called *Poun*, where their business was washing sand for gold and silver. Their queen was very fat and was called *Mena*, and they were called *Pouni*, and *Ou Mena* (Mena's men), names still applied to dwarfs in the Dra Valley. In Ta-Pount is the tomb of "the fat queen *Hlema*," or "*Hlema-Mena*," where in times of drought offerings are still made. The ruins of the old city are called by the people of Southern Morocco *Poun* or *Pount*, or *Ta-Pount*.

Two Dafour dwarfs, whom I found in Cairo lately, and who had dwarf klicks in their speech, spoke of Ta-Pount and of *Hlema-Mena*, both of which they connected with the Dra Valley and *Ta-Pount*. One of the dwarfs would not come to see me a second time, she was so horrified at my mentioning the awful name of *Didoo* ("Didoo-Osiris"); "anyone who does that is sure to swell up and die, or to wake up dumb, or blind!"[1]

The Sherif of Warzazat at the head of the Dra, in which district are the ruins of the Cyclopean city of Poun or Pount, has offered to take Mr. Harris there, who has been in correspondence as to his expedition with the Royal Geographical Society and myself. He is probably now in "*the Holy Land of Pount*," the cradle land of the Egyptian race, which Champollion, Bunsen, and other early Egyptologists identified with Mauritania

The last expedition to Pount mentioned on the monuments took place between 3 and 4,000 years ago; but Queen
Hatasu's mission to that country, so elaborately and boast-
fully portrayed, will probably turn out to have been a ro-
mance on stone. If so, the last expedition was that of the
Egyptian *Hannu* (Hanno!) between 4 and 5,000 years ago.
If there are any vestiges, however slight, of that oldest of
cities and of civilizations to be found in the Dra Valley,
the results of Mr. Harris's expedition will be of much interest to the world.

FOOTNOTE

[1] A Beni-Bacchar, at Tangier, when asked if he knew the name of
Didoo, exclaimed in surprise "How is it possible that the gentleman ever heard of Didoo? The name is old, old, very old." From
that time forth he kept away from me. He was a magician and
fortune-teller, and very superstitious.

Racial Dwarfs in the Atlas and the Pyrenees
Letter to the Editor (*The Academy*), August 5, 1893

R. G. Haliburton

A dwarf is a very little thing to get into a rage about. It was, therefore, somewhat of a surprise to me to learn from *The Spectator*, during the discussion on my paper on "Dwarfs and Dwarf Worship" in September, 1891, that there were persons in London who could not hear the subject of dwarfs mentioned without flying into a rage. Also, in January last, referring to the substantial support which recent discoveries in the Atlas had given to my views, *The Spectator* said that my theory had been "met with an acrimony of dissent which could not have been stronger if it had advocated unlimited dynamite."

Of this "acrimony of dissent"—which found vent in epithets not generally used in such discussions, such as "Gulliver," "Munchausen," etc.—we are reminded, at this late day by Mr. Stuart Glennie's letter to *The Academy*, with its significant heading, "Mr. Haliburton's Dwarfs." In it he conveniently ignored the fact that the question as to the existence of dwarf tribes in the Atlas had been practically settled by the discovery of rebel pygmies in the mountains near Morocco City by members of the Scotch Mission, an account of which appeared in *The Morocco Times* of January 26, 1893, describing the little men and women that frequented the sacred waters near the tomb of Mulai Ibrahim in the Atlas. Mr. Harris, who had heard of these dwarf tribes from the Mission, enquired at Amzmiz—a town at the foot of the Atlas, on the road to Mogador, and only two days from Morocco City, and a place well known to him, and visited by scores of Europeans every year—and was told by everyone, from the governor downwards, that there were such dwarfs in that district who would not recognize the Sultan or pay taxes; and he afterwards met fourteen of them, in all, who had a reddish complexion, and were from four feet to four feet six inches in height. His letter describing them appeared in *The London Times* of January 10. The only question now raised is as to how they became so small. The highest living authority on such subjects, Schweinfurth Pasha, whom I met in Egypt last spring, told me that he had no doubt that they were ordinary African "racial" dwarfs.

The discussion as to them in 1891 probably arose from the fact (no doubt a singular one) that the editor of *The Morocco Times*, who was then residing in London, had never heard of such dwarfs, though he had lived at Tangier for six years. His scepticism was confirmed by the statement made to him by a merchant, who had resided in Morocco City for a quarter of a century, that he, too, had never heard of these dwarfs. Yet this "old residenter" was, to his surprise, told by members of the Scotch Mission that, on enquiry, they had learned that dwarf tribes are to be found not far from the city. He afterwards mentioned the fact to Mr. Harris. It is, of course, very singular that I was the first European that had heard of these dwarfs; but no one but myself had ever asked about them, and the natives never thought of volunteering, unasked, to give any information as to them.

The lesson which this Amzmiz incident teaches us is that it is safer to trust to enquiries on the spot, or to the statements of natives of the locality in question, than to rely on the infallibility of competent authorities who have never specially looked into the matter.

As respects the existence of racial dwarfs in the Val de Ribas, in the Province of Gerona, Spain, where Catalan is spoken, a minute description of them was published in *Kosmos* for May, 1887. I wished to verify it, if possible; but I enquired in Spain—not in France, as Mr. Glennie has done. There is no English consul in France nearer to the Val de Ribas than the one at Bordeaux. I made enquiries in Madrid among scientific bodies there, and wrote to Mr. MacPherson, H.B.M. Consul at Barcelona, which is only a few hours by rail from the place in question. I did not think of asking him if he knew anything about these dwarfs in the Pyrenees, as I assumed that he had never heard or thought of them; but I asked him to make careful enquiries as to their existence. After a month or two he wrote to me that, after very careful enquiries, he was certain that there were such racial dwarfs, especially in the Collado de Tosas; and his full description of them fully confirmed that which had appeared in *Kosmos*, and also agreed with the account of similar dwarfs, with "mahogany colored" woolly hair, which an Austrian merchant, who had seen them in the market-place at Salamanca, had given me. Mr. MacPherson said that he found that the dwarfs were often confounded with cretins, but that he had fully satisfied himself that there were both cretins and dwarfs in the district in question.

Mr. Stuart Glennie has supplemented his letter by one to *Nature* of July 27, stating that he wrote to Mr. MacPherson, but received no reply. He probably wrote to him in substance what he has written to *The Academy*, that he and his French friends (none of whom probably have ever been in the Val de Ribas or can speak Catalan) might, could, would, and should have heard of these dwarfs if they really existed there. It is to be regretted that ignorance as to the existence of these dwarfs on the part of his informants, and Mr. MacPherson's avoidance of a correspondence with him, deterred him, while in the south of France, from making the easy journey he speaks of. A few hours in the Collado de Tosas would have been more useful than weeks spent with his French friends. We must hope that he will bear in mind hereafter the lesson taught by the unexpected discovery at Amzmiz; and that he will also remember that neither cretinism nor any other disease can turn ordinary Europeans into pygmies with broad, flat noses, a copper-colored complexion, and mahogany colored wool, peculiarities which can only be racial and the result of heredity.

When the argument, or rather retort, was used two years ago, "Why did you not yourself visit the country of the dwarfs?" I did not reply; but now that Mr. Glennie has revived it, I may point to it as a sample of the style of argument adopted by my critics. A year ago only I recovered my health, and partly my strength; but for ten years previously I had been an invalid, who could not "rough it" in any way, or stand the fatigue of long journeys even by rail.

But under the circumstances I did as much as Mr. Glennie, perhaps, would have done; I offered £100 to an explorer if he would visit Pount in the Dra Valley, and I also offered to pay his expenses if he would visit the Val de Ribas. I much regret that his engagements prevented him from accepting my offers.

If Mr. Glennie can give us any new information on this subject, by all means let him do so; but it is full time that his "acrimony of dissent," so unusual in such discussions, should be dropped.

Racial Dwarfs in the Atlas and the Pyrenees
Letter to the Editor (*The Academy*), August 12, 1893

J. S. Stuart-Glennie

Mr. Haliburton complains of finding that people "get into a rage about so very little a thing as a dwarf." Let me say that no competent ethnologist will be either surprised at, or indisposed to welcome, any new discovery of dwarf races. But what may not unreasonably provoke those interested in such discoveries are assertions of which the positiveness is out of proportion to the adequacy of proof, and particularly the imbedding of these assertions in a maze of other assertions of the most questionable, if not incredible, character.

As to Mr. Haliburton's attack on myself, charging me with "an acrimony of dissent unusual in such discussions," I shall only state the following facts. It was I who was asked to report in his paper offered to the Orientalist Congress of 1891, and I did so favourably. Ever since then, and no later than in *Nature* of July 27, I have publicly expressed my agreement with him as to the probable former wide distribution of dwarf races. And from private conversation and correspondence Mr. Haliburton is aware that certain theories of my own, and one particularly as to the origin of stories of fairies, would be so greatly strengthened by further additions to the evidence collected by De Quatrefages and others as to the existence of dwarf races, that such further discoveries would be welcomed by few persons more than by myself.

The very fact, however, that I have theories which would be supported by further evidence as to the existence of racial dwarfs makes me, perhaps, more critical than I might otherwise be of such evidence. Now, I have not seen the *Morocco Times* of January 26, about dwarfs in the Atlas; but I have seen the letter of Mr. Harris in the *London Times* of January 10, the evidence on which Mr. Haliburton appears chiefly to rely. And this is how Mr. Harris summarises the results of his researches: "Although, perhaps, our visit to the Atlas may tend to prove the existence of small people, it will certainly have a damping effect upon the many romances woven up with their existence"; and he then proceeds to contradict these "romances" of Mr. Haliburton's. Mr. Harris finally "finds himself forced to believe that they owe their small stature to the climatic influences and the rigorous conditions of life in the country they inhabit." And as to the dwarfs whom Mr. Haliburton believes to be living in the Wad Draa, Mr. Harris says, "I am unable even to venture an opinion." But there is clearly nothing in this to negative the existence of racial dwarfs in the Atlas; and I regret that the corrected proof of my letter in the *Academy* of July 22 was unfortunately received too late, in which I made it, perhaps, more clear that what I questioned was not so much the existence of these asserted racial dwarfs, as the further assertions as to the Egyptian "Holy Land of Punt" on the Atlantic shores of the Atlas, &c., &c.

As to the asserted dwarfs in the Pyrenees, I should have been particularly delighted to discover them, as they would have been in the most interesting relations with the Ligurian giants whose caves I had been exploring on the Riviera. Mr. Haliburton now complains that I made my inquiries in France and not in Spain. But my inquiries were chiefly made in the South of France simply because Mr. Haliburton, in his letter to *Nature* last January, located his dwarfs "within half a day's journey of Toulouse." Now he says that they are "only a few hours by rail from Barcelona." But to his informant at Barcelona I also wrote, not, however, in such a way as Mr. Haliburton groundlessly supposes, but merely asking whether Mr. McPherson had received any further information on the subject, and whether he could oblige me with some rough estimate as to the probable time required for, and expense of, my proposed journey in search of these dwarfs. To this letter, as I have said, I had no reply. Had Mr. McPherson informed me, as Mr. Haliburton now informs us, that these Pyrenean dwarfs are "only a few hours by rail from Barcelona," I should immediately have decided on the journey. But Mr. McPherson's silence naturally appeared ominous, particularly as, in his letter in *Nature*, he had admitted that the dwarfs are often confounded with Cretins, and that he had never himself visited the place, though of so easy access.

I shall only add that the facts which I stated in the *Academy* of July 22, and in *Nature* of July 27, had been withheld for five months in the hope that my extensive correspondence about these dwarfs would lead to some confirmation of Mr. Haliburton's assertions. Let the reader, therefore, judge of the "sweet reasonableness" of his charge of "acrimony of dissent."

J. S. Stuart-Glennie
United Service Club: August 5, 1893

Racial Dwarfs in the Atlas and the Pyrenees
Letter to the Editor (*The Academy*), August 19, 1893

R. G. Haliburton

It is amusing to note the great anxiety which Mr. Stuart Glennie evinces to destroy my credibility. For that purpose *The Academy* did not suffice as a medium for adequately circulating his acrimonious criticism, and he has also utilised *Nature*. As he no doubt has a profound respect for Mr. Budgett Meakin, who has been my ablest and most persistent critic, I quote the following extracts from his paper, *The Morocco Times* of January 26, 1893:

"An English resident, speaking Arabic, who has just come from the foot of the Greater Atlas, gives us important and valuable information about the stunted mountaineers who inhabit certain portions of that range hitherto unvisited by Europeans... Messrs. W. B. Harris and Cunninghame Graham have also, without reaching the limits of our present informant, met with traces of the same most interesting people [He then tries to account for their small size by a theory new to science, that living up in the mountains had dwarfed big Berbers into pygmies a good deal smaller than Andaman Islanders! Mr. Cunninghame Graham writes to me he believes they are racial; and, as I have stated, Schweinfurth Pasha thinks they are merely ordinary African dwarfs]. They may yet prove to be connected with Mr. Haliburton's little friends of the Dra Valley, some hundreds of miles away on the other side of the Atlas chain.

"The traveller whose story we have to tell was within two hours of the holy shrine of Mulai Ibrahim, the patron saint of southern Morocco, a shrine where it is believed by the credulous Moors that many miracles are daily wrought on the bodies of the sick and ailing. ... Being in the neighborhood of this celebrated saint's tomb, our friend naturally made enquiries from the natives around, and requested them to guide him to the place. This he found them unwilling to do, notwithstanding tempting offers, the Kaid of the district with his soldiers being on the alert to prevent any further advance into the mountains. Checked thus, he made other enquiries, and found the facts elicited harmonious, although coming from widely different and independent sources. One of the facts most interesting to him was that a number of small men and women were constantly to be seen in and about the saint's tomb, which they visited from a distance of one, two, or even more, days' journey from the other side of the mountains. When he questioned the truth of this, many natives around him swore by Allah that they had seen them with their very eyes. Our informant, on asking the reason why, if there were such people, they were never to be seen on the plains, and why the rest of the world was ignorant of their existence, was promptly told that a fine of $100 was imposed upon every unfortunate dwarf who was caught out of his recognised district. ... This naturally aroused his curiosity to a high pitch; and upon his servant—a trustworthy and intelligent Moor, who speaks

English and is well known to us personally—volunteering
to go and spy out the land in company with one of the Raid's
servants, arrangements were made that the two should start
early next morning. It was about noon next day when these
two spies returned. They brought with them some of the
sacred dust from the tomb of Mulai Ibrahim, and also the
following wonderful story:

"They reached the tomb after crossing the line of mountains just above their employer's camp, and a level plateau
on the other side, situated about half-way up the grand and
majestic mountain at the back ... They had also seen there
little men dressed in ordinary mountaineer garb, with
women small and pretty, handsomely dressed and decked
out with jewelry and other ornaments. These they afterwards
saw bathing together promiscuously in the sacred stream *a
la nature*. They brought back with them a string with a knot
tied in it, by which they had taken the height of one of
these interesting little men, which, on being measured,
proved to be about four feet six inches in length. The height
and build of the women were declared to be proportion-
ately smaller and lighter."

Mr. Meakin kindly sent the Moor to me, and I found the
interview an interesting one.

Mr. Harris, in December last, met at Amzmiz with a very
remarkable and exceptional instance of little rebel tribesmen, whose ancestors had probably inhabited that district
before the arrival of the Arabs, and had been for more than
a thousand years in contact with Islam. Most probably a
majority of them are Moslems. Some of them wore beards
as Moorish Moslems do. Mr. Harris, who found them hated

and dreaded by the Moors, came to the conclusion that he had before him a type of the rest of the dwarf tribes in Morocco, though nearly all of the latter live in very isolated and secluded localities, where they are safe from Moslem influences. In 1890-91 a large mass of evidence was given by natives of southern Morocco, that these dwarfs generally are not Moslems, and do not go to Mecca; but that they worship Didoo Isiri, a statement incidentally confirmed last spring by my finding at Cairo two Darfur dwarfs, who seemed to be horrified at my mentioning the awful name of Didoo, just as the Irish and Welsh and some Spanish peasants shudder when they hear anyone pronounce the name "fairy."

Mr. Harris, in a letter to *The London Times* of September 14, 1891, said of a native of Akka, "He could not in any way explain the extraordinary reticence of the Moors in speaking of them" (the dwarfs).

In his letter of January 10, 1893, speaking of the mass of statements of natives on these points (which in no way affected the main question at issue, as to the existence of tribes of dwarfs in the Atlas), Mr. Harris says: "Although perhaps our visit to the Atlas may tend to prove the existence of small people, it will certainly have a damping effect on the many romances woven up with their existence." I felt on reading this that, if it should meet the eyes of my critics, they would not hesitate to apply the word "romances" to my statements; but Mr. Harris protested against such an idea, and assured me that he did not think of me when he wrote the sentence.

Mr. Harris's closing remarks clearly show what he thinks of my labors and myself, and Mr. Stuart Glennie therefore takes care not to quote them.

"Having now clearly shown that tribes of abnormally small stature inhabit the upper peaks of the Atlas, there yet remains to be proved the question of the pygmies of Wad Dra, and many most interesting subjects pertaining to their existence. The fact that Mr. Haliburton's statement of *the existence of a small race in the Atlas Mountains* met at the time with much denial and a considerable amount of scoffing, and *has now been shown to be true,* renders it not improbable that in time the rest of his researches into the questions of southern Morocco may equally be confirmed."

Dwarfs in the Pyrenees

Letter to the Editor (*The Academy*), August 26, 1893

David MacRitchie

I have read with interest the letters by Mr. Haliburton and Mr. Stuart Glennie on this subject; and if the question has not already been sufficiently discussed, I venture to add a few remarks of my own. My reason for doing this is that, whereas neither of these gentlemen, nor the Consul at Barcelona, nor, apparently, the majority of Mr. Glennie's correspondents, if not all of them, have seen any specimens of the dwarfs referred to by Mr. Haliburton, it has been my lot to encounter two or three of them. My information is very meagre, but it is to the following effect.

Some years ago I spent six or seven weeks in French Catalonia (Roussillon), in the Valley of the Tech. The time was winter, and I was there chiefly for the benefit of my health; consequently, my walks were limited in their range. One day, however, as I was following the path which, skirting the "foot-hills" of the Pyrenees, leads from Amélie-les-Bains to the small town of Arles-sur-Tech, I heard a hoarse cry on the hillside above me, and, on looking up, "was ware of" a grotesque dwarfish figure hastily descending a ravine that eventually joined my path. His height—for the dwarf was a male—was somewhere about four and a half feet. But as to that, and the exact shade of his complexion, which, I think, was decidedly darker than that of the surrounding peasantry, I have only my memory to trust to, and cannot speak with absolute certainty. As he drew nearer, I felt less and less inclination to make his acquaintance. He was obviously an imbecile, and his ugly face wore a sullen and even threatening expression. Such language as he possessed was presumably Catalan, of which I only knew a few words. So I let him go on his way without attempting to speak to him. If I remember rightly, he was carrying a pack of some kind, and had a staff in his hand, and he was making for Arles by a cross road. Some days later, I saw another dwarf of similar appearance, at a town farther down the Tech Valley. And on a third occasion, when I was driving with a Catalan gentleman in the same neighbourhood, we passed a male dwarf who may or may not have been one of those two. In answer to a question of mine, my friend merely dismissed him with some such word as *crétin* (it was not "*crétin*," however, though he was speaking French). He evidently did not regard the subject as interesting, and I did not pursue it further. But he impressed me with the idea that he did not understand this dwarf to belong to a separate race.

These, then, were presumably examples of the "goitreus de petite taille" indicated by Mr. Glennie's correspondent; for, although they had no strongly-developed *goître*, they were undoubtedly of the *crétin* type. But, on the other hand, they were dwarfs, and equally supported Mr. Haliburton's contention. For my own part, I should be disposed to say that they represented a racial type. I find it very difficult to

believe that any inherited or acquired diathesis could trans-
form some members of the handsome Catalan people into
those imbecile dwarfs. Indeed, this consideration raises the
whole question of cretinism. One ethnologist (whose name I
forget, and I am at present too far from libraries to ascertain it)
has boldly asserted that the *crétin* is simply a "throw-back"
upon primitive man; and the occurrence of the type in certain
districts would thus mean that primitive tribes had survived
longer in those districts, and that the occasional appearance of
a *crétin* in the general population signified an inheritance
of some of that blood. Certainly, when I think of those
Pyrenean dwarfs, and of others that I have seen in Switzerland and Hungary, they seem to me akin *to each other*, and not
to the surrounding populations. This idea is interesting. Dr.
George Macdonald has a gruesome story of a noble family
in the north-east of Scotland, whose last representative, by
a freak of atavism, did not resemble any of his ancestors
for many centuries, but was "a primaeval savage" (locally
described as an "etin"), a ferocious cannibal who, one day
when his keeper was off guard, snatched a baby from its
mother's arms and plunged it into the seething broth-pot.
The same idea is present in another novel, which is based
upon the humorous incident of a young married couple—
white people, but of whom one had inherited negro blood
through a remote ancestor—who were suddenly staggered
by finding themselves the parents of a black child. Both
this young "negro" and the Scotch "etin," therefore, while
of immense rarity in the general stock, represented distinct
racial types; and were not mere "sports" of nature. So, also,
is the *crétin*, according to one ethnologist at least.

However, the question as to whether the Pyrenean dwarfs are racial or not could be settled to Mr. Stuart Glennie's satisfaction by a visit of two or three days. He would find the town of Gercna well worthy of a visit; and I fancy the Collado de Tosas is within "striking" distance of it; perhaps the Val de Ribas also. Or, one might cross from the French side, going up to Cérét from Perpignan by rail, and thence walking or driving for a couple of days. I do not suppose that there is any very large colony of dwarfs, *crétins* or not, in the eastern extremity of the Pyrenees; for the fact would then have been settled long ago beyond dispute. But the distinct accounts quoted by Mr. Haliburton, combined with my own casual experience, lead me to believe that there are still many representatives of an ancient dwarf type in that locality.

David MacRitchie
Frenich, Loch Tummel, N. B.: August 18, 1893.

Survivals of Dwarf Races
in the New World

R. G. Haliburton

It may be well to explain that the word *Pygmy* is merely a nickname for a dwarf. The old English form of it is like that in use among the Arabs, "a Thumb," *i.e.*, as "high as your Thumb," a "Tom Thumb," a "Hop-o'-my-Thumb." In Greek it was *Dactyl*, "a finger."

As only three years have elapsed since the announcement of the existence of dwarfs south of the Atlas was made, and two years only have passed since I drew attention to dwarfs in the Pyrenees, a few preliminary remarks may be necessary before discussing the subject of survivals of a dwarf race in America very similar in many respects to those of the Atlas and the Pyrenees.

Till Schweinfurth's great work, "The Heart of Africa," appeared in 1873, it was assumed that the Pygmies were mythical, and when he described a regiment of them which he saw among the Mombuttu, near the Albert Nyanza, he was derided by not a few as an impostor.

Eighteen years later my statement that a very similar race existed in the vast region between the Sahara and the Great Atlas, was vehemently denounced, and in acrimonious editorials the "Times" and the "Standard" criticized my paper on "Dwarfs and Dwarf Worship," read before the Ninth Congress of Orientalists (1891).

The Congress awarded the author of the paper a medal.

Professor Sayce, one of the most eminent Orientalists of the age, wrote subsequently, "Your name will be henceforth attached to the discovery of dwarf races in North Africa, as Schweinfurth's has been to that of the dwarfs of Central Africa. I wonder if your dwarfs have anything to do with the Neolithic people, who carved the forms of animals, birds, and men on the sandstone rocks of North Central Africa, when the Sahara was a fertile plateau."

A year later the conclusions come to in my paper were unexpectedly verified by an *a fortiore* argument, based on the discovery not only of a dwarf tribe residing in the high ranges of the Atlas almost in sight of Morocco City, but also of a pygmy race far to the north of Morocco, in the Eastern Pyrenees and other localities in Spain.

This fact was also for a time disputed by a writer in the Academy, but no one now questions it. Mr. David Mac-Ritchie, the well-known authority on the Ainos and the little "underground people," and builders of so-called "Fairy mounds," "Picts Houses," etc., in North Britain, was induced in May last by me to visit the Eastern Pyrenees, and his account of the little people that he saw there will soon appear. In May also I succeeded, after a two years' search, in procuring a paper in Spanish by Professor Miguel Morayta giving a very clear and precise account of the Pygmies of the Val de Ribas, who, he says, are looked on by their Catalan neighbors as belonging to a distinct race, and are called by them "foreigners," or "wonders" (*fenomenus*), as well as *Nanos* or *Nanus*. He says that they have Mongolian or Tartar eyes, square flat faces, and flat broad noses, and are from 4 ft. to 4 ft. 8 in. in height. A majority of them, when they reach 24 years of age, suffer from *goitre*, and are called Cretins, but Cretinism does not attack their larger neighbors, who for many centuries have lived near them. Cretinism, in the Pyrenees and the Alps, it seems to me, is *racial* in its character, and is not a *disease*, but a *symptom* of decadence in a moribund race of dwarfs, who in the recesses of mountains are slowly going through the process of *dying out* through failing vitality, just as many centuries ago their race must have died out on the plains of Europe and Asia.

This can, I think, be easily accounted for by the fact that everywhere dwarf races are born hunters, and therefore flesh eaters, who, when deprived of their nutritious food by being driven from their hunting grounds, in time lose their superabundant vitality and agility, and die out, just as plants and trees do when the soil no longer supplies them with proper nutriment.

I now turn to the subject of the survival of an early dwarf race in the New World, which from like causes may have also died out nearly everywhere. The natives of Hispaniola told the companions of Columbus that the first created race were dwarfs, who were feeble and died out, and became Cemis or guardian spirits.

In 1888, only a few months after my hearing of the Atlas dwarfs, I was told by the governor of St. Helena of a Chinese-looking little race that invaded British Honduras in 1882. I subsequently tried in vain to get some further information as to them, until I asked a Guatemalian general, with whom I crossed the Atlantic, if he knew anything about them. He informed me that he had commanded an expedition against them; that they were Pagans, and very savage, and would neither give nor accept quarter, and that in consequence of the danger of keeping them prisoners, they were always shot when captured by his men; that they were from four feet to four feet six inches in height, had human sacrifices, and used poisoned arrows, and blowpipes. A point of special interest relating to them deserves mention;—There seems everywhere to be an hereditary aptitude for plaiting, or weaving mats, etc, in dwarf races, such as the Andaman Islanders of the Indian Ocean, the dwarfs of Southern Morocco, and in some places the Nanos of Spain, whose occupation is "making mats of Esparto grass;"—the "Panama hats," of world-wide fame, are not made at Panama, but on the river *Garrion*, on the frontier of British Honduras, by these dwarfs.

A dwarf tribe in Southern Morocco is called *Ait Geronan*. In 1882, in a paper read before the A. A. A. S. by myself, on "Mount Atlas and its Traditions," I mentioned that the story of Hercules stealing the flocks of Geryon came from Southern Morocco. It is interesting to note that the Egyptians and the Greeks often represented Hercules as a dwarf, and that the Spanish Nanos principally reside in the province of *Gerona*, and not far from the district and the head waters of the Garonne. The scene of this myth is supposed by some ancient writers to have been in the eastern Pyrenees.

After my Guatemalian informant reached Europe I endeavored in vain to get further information from him. Last year, however, on making inquiries as to these dwarfs at the Colonial office, I was told of a gentleman named Mr. Blancaneaux, who had lived among them, and who afterwards wrote me a long letter giving me much information, but, unfortunately, when I wished to get further details, I found he had returned to his home in the interior of British Honduras.

He said that he had heard of the expedition of my Guatemalian informant, but that he believed that the origin of the trouble had been in promising the savages too much, and performing too little. He gave them a very high character, and said that there need be no difficulty with them so long as they are justly and truthfully dealt with. He described the height of the Mayagan as "for the most part five feet and under," but he did not specify the exact height of the Lacouton, though he spoke of them as "of the same stamp."

As my Guatemalian informant described the Lacouton as from four feet to four feet six, and Sir William Flower says that a race that does not exceed five feet three inches in height may be classed as a dwarf race, and as apparently none of these people are larger than the Andaman Islanders or the Bushmen, there can be no question that they are true dwarfs.

The *Mayagan*, so called from their having come from the Maya country, Yucatan, cultivate the soil and use firearms, but the warlike *Lacouton*, of whom the Guatemalian general spoke, use only poisoned arrows and blowpipes. They are also called *Masewal*. [A dwarf tribe of the Kalahari Desert, South Africa, is called *Masawar*.] They are redder in complexion than the Mayagan. Mr. Blancaneaux lays that all the tribes that he has seen are more or less mixed with the blood of the Lacouton, who are of the same stamp as the Mayagan. They live near the dividing line between Guatemala, Yucatan, and British Honduras. Like other dwarf races, they have a prominent abdomen, and have eyes resembling those of the Chinese, a peculiarity which is observable in nearly all dwarf races. They have, too, a knowledge of plants, and of the healing art, which also is a part of the traditionary lore of pygmy races. The incantations and dances of the Cinghalese Veddahs (called "Devil dancers") are almost precisely the same as those practised by South African dwarfs.

Are M. de Charnay's "Lacondon" of Yucatan, whom he describes as of medium height, the same as the Lacouton of British Honduras? Perhaps Mr. Blancaneaux's "Lacouton" should have been read "Laconton." The description of them, however, by the Guatemalian General has been indirectly confirmed, in more than one particular, by the account given by Mrs. Le Plongéon, in her "Up and down Yucatan," of the capture by wood-cutters, "near the frontier of British Honduras," of a very small dwarf woman, (oddly enough) described by them as "wearing a large hat." In the hope of getting a sight of her tribesmen, the woodcutters sent her back to them with presents.

"The buildings on the Eastern coast, and on the Islands of Mujeres and Cozumela give evidence of habitation by a diminutive race. 'Tradition among the Indians refers frequently to the Aluxob (pygmies), and they ascribe all the monuments to them.'" (See *Proc. of American Antiq. Socy.*, Ap. 24th, 1874, p. 71.)

The "Illustrated American" (N. Y.), of Sept. 22, 1894, announces that that enterprising paper is about to send a party to explore those curious ruins on the Andes known as "the city of the Pygmies."

Mr. A. H. Gatchett, in his "Ethnographic Sketch of the Klamath People" (contributions to N. A. Ethnology, Smithsonian Institution, vol. II. p. 1, xcix.) says: "Miraculous dwarfs are mentioned under the name of *Nahnias*, whose footprints, as small as a child's, are sometimes seen on the snow-clad slopes of the Cascade Mountains. But the dwarfish creatures who make them can only be seen by those who are initiated into the mysteries of witchcraft, and who by such spirit-like beings are inspired with a superior knowledge, especially in their treatment of diseases." "Another dwarf genius, about four feet high, lived on Williams River. The Klamath appear to know certain spirits of diminutive size, but the characteristics of such are not distinct enough to permit identification with the fairies, Erdmännchen, or Kabeiroi, of European mythology." These, however, I have shown were originally dwarfs. The oldest and most venerable institutions of antiquity were "the mysteries of the Cabiri," and the oldest God of Egypt, the Creator, Ptah, was a dwarf, and is called *"the Revealer."*

It cannot be a mere coincidence that at Uxmal, only a few hundred miles from the region to this day inhabited by the dwarf Lacouton, and Mayagan, we find that one of the finest specimens of American architecture is called *"the House of the Dwarf."* The legend connected with the building carries us back to the Egyptian dwarf God Ptah, for in it we are told of a dwarf Deity, who was born of an egg.

Ptah, however, gives "the egg of creation" to Knum, who out of it fashions the world.

All this points to the existence of a dwarf race in early ages in the New World, who were objects of veneration, as was the case in the Old World. This view is confirmed by numerous representations of dwarfs recently brought to light by the explorations conducted by the Peabody Museum.

One of these is so remarkable that it is deserving of note. The face is square and broad and flat. The eyes are Mongolian; the cheeks bulge out so that they are more prominent than the nose, which is broad and flat. The resemblance of this dwarf to the Nanos described by Professor Morayta can hardly be accidental. "Their height [he says] is about four feet, or one metre and ten or fifteen centimetres. ... They are very broad cheeked, which makes them look stronger than they really are. In general they all walk inclined forward. ... Their features are so characteristic that when we have seen one we think we have seen them all. They all have a red complexion, and red hair, but like that of a peasant who does not comb or take care of his hair. They have a round face that is as wide as it is long, but the cheek bones are very prominent, and the jaw bones strongly developed, which makes their faces seem square. To this square look the nose contributes. It is flat and even with the face, which makes it look like a small ball, and the nostrils are rather high up. The eyes are not horizontal, the inside being lower than the outside, and they look like the Chinese, or rather like the Tartar race. To this must be added that they have no beard, four or six hairs, not of a beard but of down, being all they have on their face. Their faces are fleshy, but flaccid to such an extent that they seem to have no nerves, which causes a good many wrinkles, even when they are young. To make it clear, I might say that these people have the face of an old woman. The men and women are so alike that I could not help thinking of the tradition that the Chinese men were recommended to dress differently from the women. If the *Nanus* were all to dress alike, it would be difficult to tell the men from the women. Their very large mouth helps to give them a strange appearance, with their very thick lips, which never cover their long and strong teeth. Their incisors are remarkable for length and strength. Their lips are always wet, as if they had too much saliva, which to my mind makes them very repulsive. ... It may prove that the existence of this race at Ribas may end in showing that in very remote ages there existed in Europe a Tartar race which hitherto has not been discovered."

It is a curious coincidence that Professor Putnam, in sending me a photograph of this dwarf (a sculpture in limestone), which is here reproduced, calls its subject *"a dwarf woman."*

It will be noticed that the familiar sign of the T (Tau) cross is on the forehead. It was evidently a symbol of safety and of healing, and it is still the badge of "the medicine man" in Northwestern America. Ezekiel uses the word "tau" when he says that those will be saved from the destruction he predicts, who have the "tau" (in our version 'sign") marked on their foreheads. The early Dutch writers on the Cape of Good Hope, describing a species of worship among the Hottentot Bushmen, said that they retired into a cave, and marked each other on the forehead with the sign of the cross. Mr. Lummis, in his "Land of Poco Tiempo," gives a plate of a headdress worn by women at a Pueblo festival, which is represented as having a "tau" cross on it over the forehead. [Among the Tarahumari, "with a firebrand the medicine man makes three crosses on the child's forehead, if it is a boy, and four if a girl." See *Scribner's Mag.* Sept. '04, p. 298.]

There can be but little doubt that before long dwarf tribes will also be found to exist in South America. Two years ago I was informed by Mr. Cunninghame Graham, who had lived for years and travelled much in the Argentine provinces, that it was believed there that there are dwarf tribes living on islands in a vast lake in Uruguay at the head waters of the La Plata. I am reminded of this by the statement of a friend, that about 1869 he saw an article in a magazine which described that lake, and stated that occasionally portions of floating islands have drifted down the La Plata, bringing sometimes wild animals with them, and on one occasion a dwarf family.

The description given by a traveller at the World's Fair of a pygmy race of hunters whom he had met to the south of Brazil, and the persistent rumors, that have reached the archæologists of the Peabody Museum, of the existence of dwarf tribes and dwarf buildings on the east side of the Andes, give some confirmation to these stories.

[Note.—A paper read, almost simultaneously with the above paper, at the British Association by Professor Kollmann, described the discovery of the remains of a Neolithic race of dwarfs in Switzerland, which he supposed once populated Europe. He also mentioned the recent discovery of a Pygmy race, about 4 feet high, living in Sicily; and he conjectured that Pygmies may have been the precursors of the larger races of men.—R. G. H.]

Dwarf Klicks.—A few observations on the existence of klicks, and their connection with dwarf races, may be of interest, as it is a subject which no one has looked into except myself.

Until my discovery of these klicks in Southern Morocco, and subsequently in Spain, it had been assumed that they were peculiar to South Africa. They are simply defects of articulation, the sound of which is so peculiar that it cannot properly be described in writing.

One of them, however, which is the most common, is somewhat simple. I first heard it without suspecting what it was, when I endeavored to write down the name of the tribe to which a native of the Dra Valley, south of the Atlas, belonged. I wrote it down "Psecht;" it ought to have been "Pecht." The klick introduced a sound like "s" or " ts." I supposed that the odd spasmodic action of the tongue, with which the sound was accompanied, was the effect of some nervous affection of the throat or tongue.

Klicks in South Africa are sometimes called "Bushman klicks," for the Bushmen and Hottentots have a large variety of them, a few of which have been inherited or borrowed from them by the Kaffirs. My revered friend, the late Dr.

Moffat, the father-in-law of Livingstone, and a missionary
in South Africa for half a century, and one of the few Europeans who could pronounce them, often amused me by re-
peating them to me.

A few years ago a friend who had lived in South Africa,
and also at Mogador, the most southerly place in Morocco
accessible to Europeans, casually remarked that he had often
wondered how the Bushmen had in early times found their
way as far north as Southern Morocco, the people of which
he was convinced used "Bushman klicks."

My discovery of racial dwarfs, very similar to those of
South Africa, in the vast region between the Great Atlas
and the Sahara solved the mystery.

I have since that found that these klicks are in general
use there, and are known as "eating words," but are quite
unknown north of the Atlas.

But unexpectedly the range of these klicks was found to
extend as far north as the Pyrenees.

While I was residing in a coast-town in Morocco, a Barbary Jewess from Mogador, who understood Spanish, and
the dialect of Southern Morocco, told me that she had been
surprised at finding an old Spanish woman who "*ate her
words just like a Susi.*" I told her to find out where the old
woman had got her klicks, for though she was above the
ordinary size, I suspected that she must have dwarf blood
in her veins. When asked the question by my informant,
she said that she had got them from her "Nano ancestors."
Dwarfs are called in Spain *Nano*, or *Nanu*, and sometimes
(incorrectly) *Enano*. It turned out that she had the eyes and
face of a Chinaman, or a Tartar, and that her only child and

her grandchildren were Nanos, none of which much exceeded four feet in height, while several were less than that. At that time one of her grand-daughters, only three feet ten and a half inches high, was playing with children at the door of my hotel, and looked like a child of eight years of age, though she was over fourteen, and therefore a woman, for children at twelve or thirteen years of age marry in that country. She died in May last, and I was told that she had not grown any taller since I had seen her in 1891.

In Spain they have the same phrase that we find in Morocco for klicks,— "eating words." That klicks are not caused by any physical defect is clear from the fact that the old woman, who was brought up in the mountains of Murcia, has these klicks, while her little daughter and grandchildren, who have been brought up at a seaport, Malaga, with ordinary Spanish children, have no trace of them.

The belief of the Klamath people in the existence of mysterious dwarfs in the Cascade Range, and the occurrence of klicks in the language of a Northwest tribe described in the Smithsonian "Contributions to N. A. Ethnology," lead us to suspect that this tribe has inherited dwarf blood, or has resided in the vicinity of a dwarf klick-using people at some period of its existence.

Of course, if klicks only exist in North and South Africa and Spain, in the Old World, and yet are found in a part of the New World in connection with a dwarf race or its offshoots, it might point to an Eastern origin for the latter. But that klicks are not known to exist elsewhere is not the slightest evidence that they may not really exist, for nothing is more remarkable in the history of scientific investigation than the ignorance of even competent observers as to wayside truths that have not been sought for by them, or brought to their notice. Now that attention has been drawn to dwarf klicks, it is probable that they will be found in many ancient dialects, and especially in the languages of the dwarfish tribes that are found in Northeastern Asia.[1]

Are klicks of dwarf origin, and entitled to be called "Dwarf klicks?" But for my having adopted this assumption, I should never have known that my large-sized Mongolian looking Spanish informant was a half-breed *Nana*.

The name *Nahnias* for the legendary dwarfs of the Cascade Mountains is no doubt a corruption of the Spanish *Nano* (fem. *Nana*).

Note (1895)

At the meeting of the American Association at Brooklyn, the President, Dr. Brinton, stated that he knew of no existing dwarf races, and did not believe in their existence.

On Oct. 15, 1894, a few weeks after this, the correspondent in Mexico of the "Chicago Tribune" casually referred to the various races to be seen in the streets of the City of Mexico, among which he included,—

"Indians from the hills, and queer little dwarfish savages clad in two coarse woollen garments, who have their Hottentot-like habitations within the gates of the city, living in their huts of adobe, in settlements often found behind respectable blocks of houses, ... those strange dwarf people, who glide in and out of the crowd like gnomes."

Mr. A. Glaspell, an American who has had business in the City of Mexico, says that he saw crowds of these dwarfs, about four feet high, who had come in from the country on the 12th of December to attend the great national feast of "the Mother of the Gods," now the *fiesta* of "Our Lady of Guadalupe."

Like the moribund *Nanus* of the Val de Ribas, and for the same causes as are described on the second page of my paper, those dwarfs that live within the walls of the city must show a tendency to degenerate into imbeciles, and to die out through inanition and lack of vitality.

Mr. MacRitchie, referring to Dr. Brinton's statement, says, "Foxe, in 1661, discovered an island cemetery in the northwest corner of Hudson's Bay, in which 'the longest corpses were not over four feet long;' whereupon Foxe says, 'They seem to be people of small stature. God send me better for my adventure.'" (See "The Academy," London, Jan. 12, 1895.)

FOOTNOTE

[1] This conjecture, since this paper was read, has been singularly confirmed. Dr. Franz Boaz tells me he has noticed klicks in the speech of the Chinooks and the Western Eskimo. Another informant has heard them among the Mayas; and a Hindoo says that he was greatly surprised at hearing the odd sound produced by klicks in the speech of a dwarf tribe in the Punjaub.—R. G. H.

Dwarf Survivals, and Traditions
as to Pygmy Races

R. G. Haliburton

When it became clear in 1890, that the range of African dwarfs reached as far north as the Great Atlas, I naturally inferred that in prehistoric times their range extended even far to the north of the Straits of Gibraltar. That the Atlas dwarfs had *Klicks* in their speech, similar to those of the Bushman, was subsequently established, the people of Southern Morocco, among whom they are in vogue, calling them "eating words," a term applied in Spain to a peculiarity in the speech of Andalucians.

Folk-lore has also preserved in Northern Europe distinct traditions of an early race of dwarfs, who were magicians and cunning artificers in the bronze and later ages. "Balor of the Blows," the Vulcan of the Irish, "appeared at the forge as a red-headed little boy." The Dactyls (the "Tom Thumbs" of Crete) worked at their magic forges in the caves of Mount Ida. Little dark-complexioned smiths, and magicians are still remembered in Scotch folk-lore, as "the Brownies;" and the Welsh believe in Merlin's band of dwarf smiths, who are still to be heard busily at work, making and mending armor and weapons. *Taata*, a Berber name for dwarfs, reminds us of those dwarf magicians, the Tuatha de Danann.

It seemed most likely that there must be thousands of survivals in Europe of a small prehistoric race, and that there must be references to such survivals in periodical literature, or the publications of scientific societies. A very laborious search for days in the Parliamentary Library at Ottawa was rewarded in July, 1892, by my finding in a back number of *Kosmos* (May, 1887) a paragraph of only a few lines, entitled "The Pigmies of the Val de Ribas," mentioning a paper by Professor Miguel Morayta on a dwarf community in the Val de Ribas, in the province of Gerona, Spain. They were described as having red hair, Mongolian eyes, broad, flat noses, wide, flat faces, and prominent lips; but the paragraph neither stated where the paper had appeared, nor gave the author's address. Unfortunately the editor of *Kosmos* was dead, and *Kosmos* itself had come to an end. Dr. Leitner did his best to assist me, and wrote, but without success, to a scientific man at Barcelona. The British Minister in Spain also had an inquiry made at Madrid, but no one knew of these dwarfs, or of the paper, or its author. Later on, I found a half-breed Spanish Nana woman who had decided *klicks*, which she said she had inherited from *Nano* ancestors. She gave much interesting information about the Nanos, many of whom resided in the mountains of Murcia. Although a large woman herself, her daughter and her grandchildren were all dwarfs,—some of them not exceeding four feet in height.

Early in May, 1894, Mr. MacRitchie visited the Val de Ribas in order to verify the statement of Mr. MacPherson, lately British Consul at Barcelona, that there were racial dwarfs in the Eastern Pyrenees; and simultaneously I received from Mr. MacPherson a copy in Spanish of the long-sought-for paper of Professor Morayta, which, however, did not state whether it had been published or not. The gist of the Professor's paper, therefore, will be read with interest.[1]

These people (he says) live among a larger population of ordinary Catalans, who have resided there from a remote time, and who regard the dwarfs as a distinct race, calling them *extranys* (foreigners), and also *fenomenus*, and look down upon them as laughing-stocks. A good many of them, he says, suffer from *paperas* (goitre), which is phenomenal in some, and is called *Goll*, and the persons affected are called *Golluts*.

A medical man who has attended such cases tells him that these golls can be successfully treated by iodine.

The idea that arsenical waters cause the Nanos to become Cretins and dwarfs is refuted by the fact, that their Catalan neighbors do not suffer thus. In early youth Cretinism does not appear, but on their reaching maturity the *golls* begin to show themselves, increasing with years to the size of a small melon. "If all these Nanos had *golls*, I should infer that the *goll* was the cause of their low size and of their limited intellectual development." He thinks that those of the Nanos who have poor and scanty food die out. He adds all this "shows that the *Nanus*[2] are a peculiar race, with all the characteristics of such." Some of these people who live comfortably are intelligent enough to carry on business successfully. "These and many other instances show that their stupidity is the result of the way they live. ... It may turn out that the existence of this race at Ribas may end in showing that in *very remote ages there existed*

*in Europe a Tartar race, which hitherto has not been dis-
covered.*"

Professor Morayta's paper shows that Cretinism is *racial*;
but he does not explain very clearly the cause. That a dwarf
Turanian population once existed throughout Asia and Europe
we can hardly doubt, though survivals are only to be found
in the recesses of mountains. All over the world dwarfs are
born hunters, and therefore flesh-eaters. When their game
is destroyed, or they are driven from their hunting grounds,
they, no doubt, lose their wonderful strength and agility,
and gradually becoming moribund, go through the long
process of dying out, just as many plants have died out when
the soil or the air no longer supplied them with the necessary nutrition.

Those who suppose that Cretinism is the cause of dwarfism and of the peculiarities in looks, color, etc, of the dwarfs
of the Pyrenees and the Alps, are mistaking the effect for
the cause, and are "putting the cart before the horse." In
my paper on dwarf survivals, read at the Association last
year, I suggested that Cretinism was not a disease, but a
symptom of decadence among a racial dwarf population. I
have met with a singular confirmation of this view. Last
spring I visited some Acadian districts in Louisiana, and
learned that in the old French spoken there Cretin simply
means a "stupid dwarf," and has no reference in any way
to any disease. No doubt goitre, being especially prevalent
among the dwarf populations of the Pyrenees and the Alps,
was called "the dwarf disease," Cretinism.

The Denga dwarfs are the same now as they were five
thousand years ago, yet we do not hear of goitre among the

robust and warlike pygmies of the Great Lakes and the
Congo, who are flesh-eaters and hunters. I am persuaded
that if a child of a Pyrenean Cretin were to be fed on flesh
food, and made to lead an active life, he would never show
any trace of goitre on arriving at manhood. May not "Cretin"
be a very ancient name for a dwarf? The little Dactyls, as
we have seen, were *Cretans.*

The Professor describes the stature of the Nanos as
"about 4 ft., or one metre, 10 or 15 centimetres. The Nanu
is well formed; his foot is very small and well shaped; and
so is his hand, but its palm is much developed, whence the
fingers seem shorter and fatter than they really are. They
are very broad-cheeked, which makes them seem stronger
than is actually the case. They look like small men. In general they all walk inclined forward." This peculiarity appears also in the Ainos, and is ridiculed in the Japanese
illustrations of Mr. MacRitchie's work. Professor Huxley,
in describing "Iberian man" of glacial eras, states that he
must have walked thus, a conjecture which, even if nothing
more than a lucky guess, is interesting.

The men and women have a well-shaped calf and leg.
Their features are so characteristic that to see one of them
is to see all. Their hair, he describes as red, "like that of a
peasant who does not comb or take care of his hair." "They
have a round face that is as wide as it is long; the cheek
bones are very prominent, and the jaw bones strongly developed, which makes them look square. To this square look
the nose contributes. It is flat and even with the face, which
makes it look like a small ball, and the nostrils are rather
high up. The eyes are not horizontal, the inside being lower

than the outside, and they look like the Chinese, or rather like the Tartar race."

I lent Mr. MacRitchie a photograph which I had had taken of a half-breed Murcian Nana, with her granddaughter. The people of the coast town in Morocco, where she now lives, all noticed her Chinese look. Mr. MacRitchie has just returned the photograph, and writes that a person, not interested in dwarfs in any way, remarked, on looking at it, that he would take it for a likeness of a Chinese woman.

Professor Morayta says that the Nanos have only half a dozen straggling hairs on their face, which is discolored and flaccid to such an extent that it seems to have no nerves. Hence, even when they are very young, they have many wrinkles. "In short, they have the face of an old woman. If the Nanos all dressed alike it would be difficult to tell the men from the women. Their odd look is increased by their large mouth, which does not cover their long and strong teeth. Their incisors are remarkably long and strong, and their lips are always wet with saliva, as if from water-brash. The brutalized life they lead may explain their being so ignorant that many of them do not remember the name of their father or of the place where they live."

In 1894 a dwarf about four feet high, a native of Darfur, who has for years been living in Cairo, was brought to me. He resembled in many respects, the dwarfs of the Pyrenees. He had the same large teeth, open lips, and excessive saliva, but his walk was a roll from side to side. I did not notice his bending forward. His walk was precisely like that of *Gitano-Nanos*, which the old Murcian woman described and imitated. His color was a reddish brown. At the Hotel

Métropole, Cairo, there was another, but somewhat different dwarf, from the upper Nile region, who was quite black,
and had thicker lips. I did not notice anything peculiar in
his walk. The natives of the Atlas say that there are black
dwarfs there who are larger than the other dwarfs. Zebehr
Pasha told me in 1893 that the dwarfs of the upper Nile
region are called *Denga,* and are greatly superior to their
larger neighbors in intelligence. On the monuments two
Denga or *Deng* dwarfs are described as having been brought
to Egypt, who "danced divinely," and were more prized by
the Pharaohs than the products of Pount. One is described
as from the Holy Land of Pount, and the other from "the
Land of the Blessed Spirits," probably another name for
Pount. Maspero, in his *Origin of Civilization* (1894), calls
these dwarfs *Danka,* but the Report of the Egyptian Exploration Fund, October, 1894, calls them *Denka,* or *Denk.* One
of the names of the dwarfs of the Atlas is Ait Tinker, or
Dinka. In my paper on "Prehistoric Star-Lore" full reference is made to Denga dwarfs.

Mr. MacPherson, late British Consul at Barcelona, who
kindly made enquiries into the statements of Professor Morayta,
fully confirmed them. He said that small-pox carried off
hundreds of these Nanos a few years ago, and that they are
rapidly dying out, and he thinks that more of them are to
be found at the Col de Tosas than anywhere else. He was
satisfied that there are many Nanos who are Cretins, and
many who are not. Mr. MacRitchie spent a few days in that
country, but the weather and the roads were very bad, and
prevented his remaining there longer. There is also a village
called Aledo on the summit of a high mountain between

Carthagena and Granada, "inhabited by small people," which I wished him to visit, but he was unable to do so. Many weeks, or rather months, would be required to explore thoroughly the regions where it is said the Nanos are to be found. The British Vice-Consul at Carthagena intended to visit Aledo in 1893, but I have no tidings yet of his having made the excursion. We must hope that he will yet visit that place. Mr. MacRitchie has published an interesting paper on these Pyrenean dwarfs, in the "Internationales Archiv für Ethnographie," Leyden, in which some kodak photos of those dwarfs have been given by him.

Since my paper on "Survivals of Dwarf Races in the New World" was read at the meeting of this Association at Brooklyn, many things have come to light fully confirming my conclusions. In "The Academy" (London), Jan. 12, 1895, Mr. MacRitchie says, "Captain Foxe, in 1861, discovered an island cemetery in the northwest corner of Hudson Bay, in which the longest corpses were not over four feet long. Whereupon Foxe says, 'They seem to be a people of small stature. God send me better for my adventure.'" He has also drawn my attention to a list of the Indian tribes of the Valley of the Amazon, by Clement R. Markham, recently published by the Anthropological Institute of Great Britain and Ireland, which mentions two dwarf tribes there, the Guayazis and the Cananas, citing as his authorities, Acuñã, Castelnau, Spix and Martius, and others. But for the most important confirmation we are indebted to the ubiquitous press correspondent. Writing from the city of Mexico to the Chicago *Tribune*, Oct. 15, 1894, its correspondent, describing the various races to be seen in the streets of the city, includes "Indians from the hills, and queer little dwarfish savages, clad in two coarse woollen garments, who have their Hottentot-like habitations within the gates of the city, living in their huts of adobe, in settlements often found behind respectable blocks of houses those strange dwarf people, who glide in and out of the crowd like gnomes."

A casual authority of this sort, who only describes what he sees, and does not trouble himself about scientific theories, is really more conclusive than the observations of a specialist, however candid he may be as to his favorite study. The testimony of this correspondent has been borne out by Mr. Robert Clarke, the Cincinnati publisher, who informs me that he also has seen these dwarfs. Mr. H. V. Wills, of Boston, Mass., tells me that his attention was attracted, at a representation of a Passion play near the city of Mexico, by some very small Indians, whom he "at first took to be overgrown children. They looked more like squaws than men, and their faces were broad, flat, puffy and wrinkled."

This is the description that M. Charnay gives of the Lacondon, on the frontier of British Honduras. He does not describe their height, but says that he could not tell the men from the women, and that they had broad, flaccid, puffy faces—almost the very same words as those used by Professor Morayta as to the Nanos of the Pyrenees. Mr. A. Glaspell, an American who has had business engagements in Mexico, says that on the 12th of December, the fiesta of our Lady of Guadaloupe (the old feast of "the Mother of the Gods"), he saw many dwarfs, who were not much over 4 feet in height, and who had come in from the country.

Another important confirmation by a press correspondent is that unconsciously supplied by one who interviewed,
at Cincinnati, last autumn, the German Dwarf Operatic
Company, and who stated that he had found that these
Lilliputians all came from a district in the Black Forest,
and were *racial* dwarfs, and not mere accidents or freaks
of nature. Professor Edwards, of the Cincinnati University,
drew my attention to this subject, as to which, no doubt,
further information will come to light.[3]

I was fully prepared for some such discovery. Thirteen
years ago my attention was attracted by the name of some
cliff dwellers in Abyssinia, which Jéan Temporal, in his
translation of an early Portuguese book on that country,
calls "Vosges." As I had in 1863 suggested[4] that there must
have been a migration from Africa to Europe in early ages,
I made a note of these facts, intending some day to enquire
whether there are not traces of cliff dwellings, or cliff dwellers, in the mountainous country of Alsace, "the Vosges."
In 1892, as my friends, Admiral Blomfield Pasha, of Alexandria, and Mrs. Blomfield, were about to spend six weeks
in the Vosges, I asked them to look into the question. In a
few weeks I received a local guide-book, which more than
bore out my anticipations. In the *Guide Joanne*, Géradmer
(Paris, Libr. Hachette & Cie, p. 26), we are told that La
Schaume of Nisheim, which surrounds Wurtzelstein, it is
believed, is inhabited by a kindly disposed race of dwarfs,
who, when the herdsmen descend to the lower valleys with
their herds in the autumn, pasture their cattle, which are of
very small size, in the upper pastures, and make cheese till
the spring. Among different authorities cited is the *Foyer*

Alsacien, by Chas. Grad. Admiral Blomfield Pasha wrote me that a very intelligent fellow-traveller, a Frenchman, believed that there were many racial dwarfs in that part of Europe, and that a careful search would put this beyond question. I also made enquiries as to the "dwarfs of Sylt," which it is supposed were exterminated by the Frisians. My informant got for me the following information from the head of the Archaeological Institute of Kiel: "The people call traditionary dwarfs *Die Unterirdeschen, Alben, Wichte, die Kleine Leute,* [the Underground People, the Albs, the Wights, the Little People], and there is no end of Sagas telling about them. Our country and Sylt are full of them, and I heard some quite new to me on this occasion. They have been digging lately in several places for skeletons, and the villagers said, 'Yonder, under that village, the Little People used to live;' and in another village the people said that under a certain mount live sets of the 'Underground Folk' lived, but they only had one cauldron (caaldron) between them, and when one party was invited by the other the cauldron had to be taken for cooking. The mount was opened, and a huge cauldron was found. Now you hear of kind acts done by these little men, and again of wicked, revengeful, spiteful deeds."

Fifty years ago that intellectual giant, Jacob Grimm, was far in advance of scientific men of our day as to this question. He seems to have assumed that there was once a widely diffused dwarf population in northern Europe, and he gives in his German Mythology an immense amount of references and traditions as to dwarfs, as will be partially seen on referring to the index of that work.

In 1892-3, Professor Sergi published in the Bulletin of the Royal Medical Academy of Rome an important paper, showing that in early ages there must have been a migration of African dwarfs to the European countries bounding on the Mediterranean, and as far east at least as Moscow. He has made a comparison of the numerous dwarfs he met with in Sicily and Italy with skeletons of dwarfs found in Etruscan tombs and near Moscow—all resembling the dwarfs of the Congo.

There are really only two classes of dwarfs, one stunted and deformed in infancy through disease, and the other *racial dwarfs*, for we may safely put down to atavism cases of the Tom Thumb type hitherto looked on as "freaks of nature." Sir Geo. Humphrey, M. D., found in all the museums in France only one skeleton of a supposed dwarf "freak;" and even that, we find, was nearly a century old, and belonged to a member of a family in the Vosges, in which there were other dwarfs. (See my paper on dwarfs, in Asiatic Quarterly. July, 1892.) I find I have omitted to mention that in 1893 (*i.e.*, after I had heard from Blomfield Pasha), I learned in Morocco that, two days south of the Great Atlas, there is a high mountain called *Voshe*, the inhabitants of which are dwarf cave-dwellers, who are called Ait Voshe (the Voshe Tribe). We have seen that Jéan Temporal called a cave-dwelling tribe of Abyssinians "Vosges;" and Professor Schlichter says that the Akka dwarfs of Equatorial Africa are known to their neighbors as *Voshu*, and also *Tiki-Tiki*, names connected with the Akka dwarfs of Southern Morocco, who are also called Jed-ibwa (the "Fathers of Our Fathers"). When I asked natives of Southern Morocco,

"Have you ever heard of the name *Tiki*?" I carefully avoided using the reduplication. They all said "Yes, Tiki-Tiki, Tiiki-Tiiki; that is a name for the Little People;" and subsequently a half-breed Spanish Nano gave me the same reply. The range of *Tiki-Tiki* extends to Polynesia, where it is used for ancestral dwarf-gods, one of which, the dwarf Creator, Tiki, resembles the dwarf Creator, Ptah, of the Egyptians.[5] "Tiki" and "Tiiki," seem to be a shortening of those names for dwarfs and dwarf-gods, so familiar to the ancients, and still used in Morocco—*Patiki*, and *Patäiki*. The *Tiika-Tiika* (a name not hitherto known to anthropologists) are very small dwarfs in South Africa, who, the Kaffirs say, are a perfectly distinct race from the Bushmen. Through his tutor, Dinuzulu informed me that the Zulus have killed them nearly all off, as "they are not fit to live." The Kaffirs greatly dread them as most dangerous wizards and magicians.

Atavism is very enduring and far-reaching; and generations, or rather centuries, are not able to efface the traces of racial, or even family traits, as can be seen in family portraits. The leading family in a district in Andalucia were surprised and shocked at finding one of their number grow up, in all respects, a typical Congo dwarf. No doubt they had inherited a remote Nano strain, which, though long forgotten, had at last asserted itself.

Size, complexion, etc., point out the places where a dwarf race must have once existed. The Black Forest is probably one of these, for the manager of the German Dwarf Operatic Company says he was able there to secure the services of several very small dwarfs. Their relatives were generally of large stature. In Sicily, and parts of Italy, Professor Sergi discovered and measured a surprisingly large number of dwarfs, many of which were as small as Congo dwarfs.

The name, "Little Father," for the dwarfs of the Atlas, and sometimes in Spain for the Nanos, must have drifted as far east as Moscow, when that prehistoric migration of African dwarfs took place, of which Professor Sergi has told us, for it still survives in that strange title by which the Czar is often addressed—*Little Father*.

I may mention a fact that has been long known to me, that the names "Dwarf" and "Fairy" came originally from North Africa, where they are still in use. Ancient Greek geographers say that the farthest west part of Gætulia (southern Morocco) is inhabited by the Maurussii and Pharussii (*Mauri* and *Phari*).

I have been frequently told by Berbers that *Fari* was a name for mining dwarfs, who wash gold and silver sand. I did not notice any superstitious dread among the Berbers as to using the name, but among the Spanish half-breed Nanos it seems to excite the same horror that it does among the Irish, Welsh and Highland peasants. My Murcian informant nearly rushed from the room at the sound of the name, and begged of me never to use it again. It is evidently an "unpronounceable name." This may be a superstition connected with the belief that if you can get hold of the name of an enemy who is a magician, you can destroy his power over you. A Highlander was able once to capture a fairy wife by finding out her name. The Irish peasants will speak of "the good people," "the gentle folk," or "the gentry," or "the little people," but you cannot get them to use the word "fairy."

The name *"dwarf,"* too, is Berber. There is a town or hamlet in the Sahara, some days to the southeast of Tafilet, called *Adwarfi* (a corruption of Ait-Warfi, "the good people," "the excellent folk,") and the place is a great centre of the little *Adwarfi*. (*Razel warfi* means "a fine man"). In Spain the Nanos are called *Adwarfi*. But the old Murcian woman used the name unwillingly. Many names and subjects among the Nanos are sacred or "tabooed." She told me she knew much about the *Cabrillas* (or "the kids")— the Pleiades; but it was not lawful to speak about those stars.

Both in Scotland and southern Morocco we meet with artificial mounds, in which there are chambers. In Southern Morocco they are inhabited by dwarfs, who take into them at night their little cattle. One of my informants, a Berber Jew, told me that, when a boy, he ventured once to sleep in one of them; but that the Berbers generally are afraid to enter the small, dark passages that lead to the central chamber; and call the little entrances "rat holes."

The name *Pecht*, which is used in Scotland for a dwarf, and is more familiar to us as "Pict," is to be found south of the Atlas. A "Large Haratin " (a native of the Dra, who is descended from dwarfs) told me that he belonged to the Ait Pecht. His dwarf klick made the name sound like *Psecht*. On one occasion, without having been questioned on the point, my Spanish informant gave me an account of the dwelling places of the Nanos of Aledo, which she said were built of large stones, covered with earth, and which were evidently similar to those of the *Adwarfi* and to the Picts-Houses of Scotland.

The head of a branch of my family for centuries went by the name of Pitcur, from owning Pitcur Castle, in Forfarshire, Scotland, now a ruin. Mr. MacRitchie, at my request, visited a place near the Castle, in which, I heard, there was a small passageway leading into a hill, for I fancied it must be a *Pict-cur*, a dwelling place or enclosure of dwarfs. The idea proved to have been well founded, and he wrote to me, that it was one of the best specimens of a Picts-House that he had ever seen. He afterwards learned that he was not the first antiquary who had explored it. If there is any foundation for the wonderful legends, that tell of the oldest castles in the North Country having been built by dwarf masons, Pitcur Castle must have been their handiwork.

Professor Sayce, in his note to Herodotus (B. III, Ch. 37), connects the name of "the Creator" of the Egyptians, *Ptah*, with that of the *Pataïki*. The philological argument is confirmed by the fact, that both Ptah and the Pataïki were dwarfs. Not only in Egypt, but also in Greece, the oldest of the gods were pygmies. Venus of Cyprus was a dwarf; her son was *Pygmæus*, and her husband, Vulcan, was no doubt a Dactyl, one of the dwarfsmiths and magicians of Crete. Solden says that the Great Gods of Palestine and Syria were pygmy deities (Pataïki).

Movers, in the first chapter of his Phoenizier, says, that "that group of deities called Dactyls, Corybantes and Cyclopes, were similar to those old Germanic divinities, now known as 'Cobbolds.'" I had not seen that passage when I suggested in my paper on "Dwarfs and Dwarf worship," that they were "like our Fairies and Brownies."

The name, *Pataïki*, is still to be heard. In parts of North Africa, and probably in Syria, the Jews hold a festival towards the end of April, called "the Great Play," and also *Pataïki!* When I asked an old Syrian Jew who lives in Alexandria, Egypt, what was the meaning of the name Pataïki, he replied, "*Kabir* is God; *Kabirieim* means the large angels, and *Pataïki* the little angels." Pausanias identifies the Pataïki with the Cabiri. But the oldest sources of religious thought among the ancients were the Mysteries, and these, it is admitted, all sprang from the venerable Mysteries of the Cabiri, *i.e.*, from dwarf mysteries.

Grimm, in his German Mythology,[6] shows how widespread was the belief that the first created race were dwarfs. Hesiod says the first race of men died out, and became blessed spirits, who were the guardians of mankind. In the West Indies[7] there was a very similar belief. The mothers of the first generation all fell in love with a primeval Lothario, and deserted their children, who grew up stunted, and ultimately died, and became *Tona* (guardian spirits), and were worshipped by men.

Among the Zuni and other Pueblo Indians, the first generation of men are called "child ancestors" (their name being written variously, Koko, Koka, or Kaw-kaw). They are intercessors for rain, and initiate youths, and take an important part in certain rites. They are represented as dwarfs, and are evidently liable to hunger, judging from the amount of provisions with which they have to be supplied when they visit their descendants. Among the Klamath Indians there is a belief, that there are certain dwarfs whose little footprints can be seen in the snows of the Cascade Mountains, but who are only visible to the medicine men whom they instruct in the mysteries of the Medicine-lodge. The Micmacs have a very similar belief in little men who live in the woods, and who, if conciliated successfully by a Micmac, will give him magic lore. Among the Choctaws there was a belief that little "Men of the Woods" catch the young men and, after putting them through an ordeal of good natured teasing, initiate them. *Bopuli*, a mischief-loving Robin Goodfellow, is the *Kokopuli* of the Pueblo Indians.

Mr. J. A. Watkins of New Orleans, an old gentleman, whose father lived among the Choctaws, and who when a boy learned their language, writes me that in the first half of the century a deputation of Choctaw chiefs waited on the government agent, and begged him, as they were fearing the effects of a drought, to let his two sons, young boys from eight to ten, visit them and bless their crops. Willing to humor them, he let his sons go. When they had been taught the proper rites, they went through the ceremony so well, that a heavy shower fell next day, and they returned home loaded with presents. Dwarfs could no longer be procured to pray for rain, and the nearest approach to a dwarf was a young boy!

Others practise this pious fraud. Our little May Queen, and the Lord of Misrule of mediaeval festivities were no doubt once dwarfs. At the beginning of May, the Japanese have a little King and Queen, who are to be seen also at St. Michael in the Azores, where at Whitsuntide, amid an immense crowd of spectators, a little King and Queen are carried in state to the Cathedral, where they are in great pomp crowned by the clergy. A procession then takes place to some tables at the market-place, where they preside over the feast, in which the poor participate. In China a little girl receives the offerings to the dead. In India[8] Durga, or Kali, is represented by a little girl who sits in a "bower of leaves." In a similar bower a little child-wife in the Western Soudan receives the god *Sokar*, no doubt the same as the ancient dwarf god of the Egyptians, Ptah-Sokar-Osiris. In Egypt[9] there was a great feast at Pithom at the beginning of May, at which two little girls officiated, who were called *Urti* ("the two Queens"). Possibly they may have been two little brides for Anuk, who is so venerable a divinity, that he may be only another type of the dwarf god, Ptah-Sokar-Osiris. In the Tonga Islands Alo-Alo, the god of rain, when he visited the earth, was welcomed by a little child-wife, who presided during the festival in a leafy bower.

We find that the Atlas dwarfs and the Nanos predict the future by watching the reflection of "the Seven Stars" in a bowl. The famous cup of Nestor, supposed to have been a divining cup, had two groups of Pleiades on its handles. In modern Egypt the person who tries divination by a bowl, is always a boy. The Atlas dwarfs, who "know more about the stars than other men," drive a good business in the Balaam line, by blessing (if not by cursing). A little Ait Atta, from near Adwarfi, who was stolen from his parents and sold as a slave, but ran away and found his way to Tangier, told me in 1894 that the Little People are greatly feared by his tribe, who address a dwarf as *Sidi Baraker* ("our Blessed Lord"). "When we see them coming, we lay down our presents before us, and bow down; and they put their hands on our heads, and bless us and our crops, and take our presents, and go away."

The Bushmen claim that their primordial mothers were the Pleiades, a star group which the ancients regarded as "Royal Stars." According to Grimm, dwarfs were supposed to be "of Royal birth." Wherever we find dwarf tribes, or their descendants, there we find vestiges of the Year of the Pleiades and of a worship of those stars.

I cannot go further into this curious subject; but I may, in conclusion, suggest that there is a marvellous and puzzling uniformity in the ideas of primitive races as to festivals, magic, healing by incantations, etc., which can only be accounted for by assuming that, in the most remote prehistoric times, there must have existed an era, in which was developed a rude system of initiations, that diffused, preserved, and at the same time stereotyped, the scanty stock of star-lore, beliefs, and domestic arts of those early days.

Note.—Prof. Frederick Starr, Dept. of Anthropology, Univ. of Chicago, Translator of *Les Pygmées* by de Quatrefages, on his return from Mexico, in a letter dated 26 Sept., '95, writes me as follows:—

"Aguas Calientes is a city of perhaps 30,000 inhabitants. In a single half-hour in the market we saw seven adults who were not more than four feet high. Of one of these we have a photograph which I shall be glad to send you presently. The people of Mexico generally are small. There is an unusual amount of difference between the males and females in stature. The women therefore are generally small. But the cases mentioned above were far below the ordinary stature. The little people you mention, quoting from the *Tribune* Reporter, are certainly from *Aytzcaputzalco*, which is connected with the City of Mexico by St. Care. They are very small, retain their old dress, are reserved and very primitive. I am told that many of them live in holes in the soft tepetate rock. These are special topics which I shall study hereafter. I have Indian authority for dwarf populations near Lake Chapala in Western Mexico. ... Several Indians at Chapala tell me that there was a fiesta there nine years ago which was very well attended. Among the people were about twenty little people, representing a dwarf race living in the mountains. They are described as about a yard high. All wore knives, and were very fiery tempered. They stood no teasing from the people of the region.

I noticed an unusual amount of little people going from Puebla to their homes. We saw a hundred perhaps go from market past us, as we sat at a bridge. The little stature was marked in both sexes and most so in the women. Many adults could not have been more than thirty-five to thirty-eight inches high. ... These little people probably came from Cholula, or near there. Most of them were primitively dressed. This I find commonly among the little people. They are conservative and reserved.

Critinism occurs in the Barranea near Guadalajara. I have not looked into it. A dwarf population, the Chontales, are reported to me by Archbishop Giliar of Oajaca. They live far from him, and he has never seen them. They are said to live in holes in the ground. "Writing about *the Little God*, at Lake Chapala, he says: "There are found, in the bed of the lake, very many curious little vessels of clay and, strange to say, spoons and ladles of the same material." The schoolmaster there said: "The people that used to live here, unlike their neighbors, had a God who was little; there-fore the gifts that were made to him were little."

That once there was a numerous dwarf population throughout Mexico, is proved, he thinks, by the small size of the Mexicans.

FOOTNOTES

[1] As much of this paper was written for publication in an English periodical a year ago, some of my quotations from Professor Morayta's paper are the same as those that appeared in my paper of 1894, "Sur-vivals of Dwarf Races in the New World."

[2] This ending in *u* is probably Catalan. In Spanish a male dwarf is a *Nano*, and a female *Nana*. The people call themselves *Nanos*, not Enanos.

[3] A German tells me he has often seen dwarfs about four feet high, who came to Baden from the Black Forest.

[4] See Haliburton, *New Materials for the History of Man* (1868). pp. 14, 23 and Note, 41, 74.

[5] *Tiki* we can trace even to Peru, where, according to Santa Cruz (see Markham's *Narrative of the Rites and Laws of the Yncas* pp. 83, 84 and plate, and 88), the Supreme God, "the Creator," was called *Ticci* Ccapac (sometimes softened into *Ticçi* Ccapac), and *Tica* Ccapac, and was represented by an egg shaped symbol. He was born of a Condor's egg, and was, no doubt the same as the primordial dwarf God of the Mayas, whose temple at Uxmal was "the House of the Dwarf," and who was born of an egg (see pp. 124, 126, 135 and 142).

[6] See Staleybrass' *Trans.* II, 563-9.

[7] Kerr's *Voyages and Travels*, III, 134.

[8] Sir Wm. Jones' *Works*, IV, 132, 185.

[9] Brugsoh. "Egypt under the Pharaohs," II, 347.

Recent Investigations
as to Pygmy Races

R. G. Haliburton

A new factor in solving the problem of human origins will hereafter be the worldwide range of Tiki (or Tiki-Tiki), as a name not only for dwarfs, but also for dwarf Creators, the Egyptian dwarf Creator Ptah, (a name connected with Patæki or Pataiki), the Polynesian Dwarf Creator, Tiki, and the Creator of the Peruvians, Ticci Ccapac.

Born of a condor's egg, Ticci-Ccapac resembles the dwarf God of the Mayas, who was also born of an egg, and whose temple was "the House of the Dwarf" at Uxmal. From "the Egg of Creation" of the Egyptian Dwarf God, Ptah, the universe was fashioned by his seven dwarf architects, the Knummu.

In my paper on "Dwarf Survivals and Traditions as to Pygmy Races," before the American Association last September, it was pointed out that the name Tiki is not confined to the Akka, or Tiki-Tiki of Equatorial Africa, but is found in the Atlas and also among the Nanos of Spain. It seems now that the range of Tiki is much wider than I had stated. The smallest tribe of Bushmen is called Tiika-Tiika. Far North of Spain we find the Tucke-Kobbolds of Germany; and still farther North, we read of Thekr and Nain, two of the primordial dwarfs forty-nine in number, 7x7?, that, according to the Icelandic Voluspa, were created before mankind.

In America, too, the range of Tiki is wider than I had supposed. Thus two of the most important little Ko-ko, or Child-Ancestors of the Pueblo Indians, are called Soo-tiki. The Araucanians (Chili), who, like the Peruvians, worshiped the Pleiades, called the Supreme Being Toqui. Among the Kaffirs he is Tiquo, a name borrowed from the Bushmen, whose primordial mothers were the Pleiades, and who at the rising of those stars dance and sing, "Oh, Tiqua, Father above us, send us rain!"

Many years ago, Professor Tylor, in his valuable work, "Primitive Culture," p. 283, identified the dwarfs of Northern folklore with a prehistoric dwarf population; and Professor Wyss has taken a similar view of the traditionary dwarfs of the Alps, who he supposes were dwarf tribes forced to take refuge there by larger neighbors.

> "For then also in the country
>   The good dwarflings still kept house,
>   Small in form, but highly gifted,
>   And so kind and generous."— Muller.
> (See Keightley's *Fairy Mythy.*, Bohn's *Antiq. Library*, p. 264-5.)

Professor Wyss' conclusions have recently been confirmed by Professor Kohlmann's discovery of the bones of Pygmies there, and by Professor Serg'i's conclusions as to a migration of African dwarfs to Southern Europe and to Russia, who resembled the Tiki-Tiki, or Akka of Equatorial Africa.

In America we meet with traditions as to similar dwarf races. My inference that Ticci, one of the names of the Creator of the Peruvians, showed that he was a Dwarf God, has been confirmed by a point which Mr. Stansbury Hager has suggested, that "the Indians of Chincha (Peru) believed that their country had been previously inhabited by a population of dwarfs, whose bones they found in tombs. (Cieza de Leon, chap. 74, quoted in Spencer's Sociology.)"

Professor Tyler conjectures that there must also have been in North America a dwarf population, as evidenced by diminutive stone cysts that have been found: and he cites as his authorities Squier, *Aboriginal Monuments of State of New York*, p. 65; also Long's *Exped*. I. 62, 275. To this day the Iroquois say that in their former raids on the Cherokees, they met with a tribe of dwarfs, very numerous, and living in caves, and though small, stronger than ordinary men. (See Erminnie J. Smith's paper on the Iroquois, *Report of Bureau of Ethnol*. 1880-'81.)

In the April number of the "North American Review," Professor Starr's paper on "Pygmy Races of Men," gives an outline of what was accomplished in this field of research up to the publication of *Les Pygmées* by Quatrefages in 1887, a work of which he is the translator. He mentions, then, the announcement by myself at the Bath Meeting of the British Association in 1888 that there were dwarf tribes in Southern Morocco. This subject was more fully discussed at the 9th Congress of Orientalists (1891), in my paper on "Dwarfs and Dwarf Worship," to which a medal was awarded; and he refers to my investigations since then tending to show that there are survivals of Dwarf races in the

Pyrenees, and also in the New World. He also gives confirmatory facts observed by him in 1895 in Mexico, and adds: "The question as to whether there are Pygmy races in America, seems to be really propounded."

According to the *Times-Herald*, of Chicago, April 26, 1896, Professor Starr's recent visit to Mexico and Guatemala, where "he was not looking for Pygmies particularly," has not contributed any new confirmatory evidence on the subject: but "he is strongly inclined to the belief that there are Pygmy tribes in Mexico and Central America, and intends to pursue his investigations in this direction, as in others, when he returns to that country next fall."

From what Professor Starr has observed, it seems plain that the Mexicans are a mixed race, with a large infusion of Dwarf blood. Not only is their stature small—in some localities notably so—but their women are still smaller. "The women in many towns would warrant us in calling the place a town of Pygmies. The men of those towns would not warrant the term. In many families where both parents are little, the children of ten or twelve years are larger than either parents."

This is what occurs among the Spanish Half-breed Nanos, as is plainly shown by a photograph which I have of a large Chinese looking half-breed Nana from Murcia, and her grand-daughter, whom I met with in a coast town in Morocco. The latter was only 3 feet 10½ inches high: *i.e.*, much smaller than an Andaman Islander; and though of full growth, she dressed like, and passed for, a child. She adopted long dresses soon after the photograph was taken. She and her grand-mother were described in 1894 in my paper on "Survivals of Dwarf Races in the New World," in the *Proceedings* of the American Association for that year; also in my paper on "Dwarf Survivals, and Traditions as to Pygmy Races," read last year before the same society.

It seems that the most important authority on the existence of dwarf races in Mexico is President Dias. "The word Chontales has two meanings. It is used to designate a race of people, and it is also used to indicate anything strange or foreign. So when President Dias, on a military excursion into wilder Mexico, saw some unusually small people, and asked who they were, the reply was 'Chontales.' He accordingly concluded that the Chontales were a race of dwarfs, and so informed the Archbishop of Oaxaca." It is to be hoped that before long some explorer will ascertain where this Pygmy tribe was seen by President Dias, and will visit them.

I regret that all my efforts have failed to get information from British Honduras as to the correctness of General Granada's estimate of the height of the Lacondon tribe of hunters, some of whom live in Guatemala, while others are within the limits of British Honduras. My correspondent there, Mr. Blancaneaux, did not reply to my letter asking for further information on that point; so, backed up by a letter from the Secretary of State for the Colonies, I wrote in 1894 to Sir Alfred Molony, the Governor, stating what I wished to find out and enclosing an open letter for Mr. B., to be forwarded to him. Since then I have heard nothing on the subject—though I subsequently sent Mr. B., by post registered, a letter and my paper on "Dwarf Survivals in the New World." This will show how much trouble I have taken, and how much difficulty I have sometimes had in getting precise data on this subject.

The latest contribution respecting Dwarfs, is a very interesting paper on "The Pygmy in the United States." by J. Wier, Jun., M. D., in the *Pop. Science Monthly* for May, describing numerous communities of descendants of African Pygmies, survivals of those victims of the slave trade, the dwarf tribes that were once to be found on the West Coast. He contends that all pygmy tribes have sprung from a common stock; and that in the remote past, when Africa was connected with Australia by land, they wandered to what are now the islands of the Pacific. May not an archipelago farther East, but now submerged, have been the bridge by which Tiki-Tiki found his way to America?

If the Akka or Tiki-Tiki, who spread over Polynesia and America, were the same Race of dwarfs, who, according to Professor Sergi, wandered North to Europe and Russia in early ages, this will explain why some Melanesian customs and festivals strangely resemble those of Europe. (See on this point, Haliburton, "New Materials for the History of Man." 1863, pp. 8-11, 18-25, 30-32, 41, 57-58, 91-98.)

Romilly was surprised at finding in New Guinea our "Jack in the Green," in Melanesian Duk-Duk, or Duka, a word which means the spirit of a dead man, or a charm worked by his aid. When a Gypsy "casts a spell" on a man, he is said to "duka him."

I was not aware, until I heard from McRitchie, that in the *Verhandlungen der Berliner Gesellshaft fur Anthropologie,* &c., (session of July 20th, 1895), Professor Virchow discussed my papers very fully, and with "sympathetic remarks."

These, coming from him, are important, for, in addition to his pre-eminent position in science, he is a special authority on the subject of Pygmy races.

In my next paper I shall mention many curious proofs that have unexpectedly "cropped out" in the course of these researches, as to "the Influence of Pygmy Races, and their Star-lore on Early Initiations and Cults."

Extracts from Mr. Haliburton's Writings

Professor Rudolf Virchow

The Dwarf Races of Morocco and Spain

The writings which have come to my hand consist of a some-what large number of shorter and longer communications, which in a somewhat varied manner, partially in chronological order, partially in the order of matter, give the testimonies obtained respecting the existence of dwarf races, or, as the writer says, of 'racial dwarfs,' in the Atlas country. A copious re-statement of these testimonies, which must have been of great value, since the writer had yet to combat with the unbelief of his countrymen, appears for the present unnecessary, since a large number of unexpected testimonies have come up to vouch for the correctness of his statements. Of course it was long before a kind of certainty had been acquired, for after the writer first learned through a man from Sus of the existence of 'a small people' in southern Morocco, it was almost ten [six?] years before a European became convinced, through autopsy, that the question related not merely to a few scattered dwarfs, but to a whole tribe. Many a credible statement had already drawn attention to a desert district situated on the south side of the Great Atlas, between the Dra Valley and the

Sahara, separated from Sus by the Lesser Atlas, and which is called by a peculiar name, 'Akka.' The people there were also called by that name long before Schweinfurth's attention had been drawn to the Akka on the Upper Nile. Here it may be added that, according to other statements, the western Akka belong to the tribe Ait Wakka. ... The small Haritin are called Baraka, also Ulad Mebrok, while the name Nezeegan is said to be used only in connection with the dwarf tribe which inhabits the town Nezeeg, near Sus.

Mr. Haliburton did not go into this region, which seems to be inaccessible on account of the turbulent character of its population. Mr. Harris, with Mr. Cunninghame Graham, followed up the statements of the Scotch Mission (at Morocco City), and he succeeded in getting sight of fourteen dwarfs in Amzmiz. His report in The Morocco Times of 26th January, 1893, is reproduced in The Academy of 19th August, of the same year. Amzmiz is a town on the way to Mogador, only two days' journey distant from the capital. In the neighborhood is found the tomb of a saint, Mulai Ibrahim, to which the people resort from a distance. Here some explorers saw the small folk, men and women, who were bathing naked in the holy stream. It appears, however, that not a single European has entered the land of the dwarfs yet.

The statements of all eye-witnesses as to the physical condition of these dwarfs agree. Their height is given as 4 ft. 6 in. from 4 ft. 2 in.; also 'not higher than four feet.' 'The women are the size of a little girl; men with beards, that of a small boy.' They have a peculiar reddish complexion 'like that of the Redskins of America'; quite different from that

of the Moors, Arabs, blacks, etc., according to others of a
'mahogany color.' They are broad and muscular; their hair
is 'crisp and curly,' 'short, woolly, like that of the blacks.'
In appearance they are so much alike that it is difficult to
distinguish one from the other. They speak the Shilhach
language of southern Morocco (Schloh), but with klicks.
According to one statement there are said to be more than
1,000 of them at the River Dora (or Didu); in other places
1,500, etc. As Leo Africanus calls Dra 'Dara,' the writer
thinks that the Darae, or Gaetuli-Darae, who are said to
have lived on the Steppes of the Great Atlas, and who were
regarded as belonging to the Libyan race, may have been
related to them.

I pass over the statements respecting names of places
and tribes, which nearly every witness has given somewhat
differently. The fact that south, and to some extent on the
heights of the Atlas a dwarf race is living, that has woolly
hair and a reddish complexion, seems to be beyond doubt;
and we must certainly give the credit of that discovery to
Mr. Haliburton, who first proved the existence of these
dwarfs.

THE RUINS OF FOUNT IN DRA VALLEY

A special interest is due to the discovery of these dwarfs
through the manifold references which the writer has tried
to harmonize with old Egyptian traditions, an endeavor in
which no less an authority than Professor Sayce stands by
him.

Mr. Haliburton found that the old Egyptian god 'Didoo,'
which Brugsch is said to have called a Nubi-Libyan Deity,

must have originated south of the Atlas, where rivers and tribes bear the name (the River Did, or Didan, Ait Didi, Ait Hedidoo, Ait Doodoon, Did, a source river of the Dra, and the River Didoo, or Dora). The god Didoo-Osiris is said to be known in that region as Didoo-Isiri, and in the Dra Valley are said to be found the ruins of an old town of image-worshippers called by the natives Ta-Pount, also *Anibna Didoo* (the Town of Didoo). Thus the query arose: Should 'the Holy land of Pount' of the Egyptians be looked for here, and not at the Indian Ocean?

The statements of Mr. Haliburton about Ta-Punt (Arab, Tabount) are somewhat obscure. It appears that the ruins lie in the upper Dra Valley, in the district of Warzazat. In them are found small figures with horse or bull heads, which are called Beni Mahkerbu, Bent Hazor, and Beni Kerbu; and also Patiki, just as the small people are called. These figures are said to be 18 inches to 2 feet high, half human, half animal, some with the body of a human being, and the head of an ape, or dog. The small people adore Didoo-Isiri. In ancient times there was a treasure of gold buried in Pount.

Professor Sayce reminds us that Schiaparelli discovered a grave near Contra-Syene, in which an inscription says that Hurkhuf, therein buried, had been sent by Pepi II. (sixth dynasty) on an expedition to the south, and that he had brought back from the king of Ammaan, among many other kinds of gifts, 'a Denga dwarf from out of the Land of the Holy Spirits, who could dance divinely, like the Denga dwarf which the late Chancellor Urdudu brought from the Land of Pount in the time of King Assa (sixth dynasty).' This expedition was one thousand years earlier than that of Hannu, which itself is to be placed one thousand years before the celebrated expedition of Queen Hatasu. The latter, however, took quite a different direction from that of Hannu, which was towards the west, 'The Holy West,' 'The Land of Truth.'[1]

Already Bunsen searched for this Put or Pount in Mauritania.[2] Mr. Haliburton brings also the story of Jonah and the Perseus Mythus in connection with that country.

In Ta-Punt is said to be the grave of 'the Fat Queen' Hlema, or Hlema Mena. Even now the dwarfs of the Dra Valley are called Puni, or Ou Mena ('Mena people'). Two Dafur blacks, whom the writer saw in Cairo, spoke of Ta Pount and Hlema Mena; and the name Didoo inspired them with dread. (He does not recall the Carthaginian Dido).

Dwarf Survivals in Spain

Finally, Mr. Haliburton also claims that survivals of dwarfs exist in Spain, both in the Pyrenees and in other parts. He appeals to explorations of the British consul at Barcelona, Mr. Macpherson, who found in the eastern Pyrenees, in the Val de Ribas, people of 1 m. to 1.17 m. in height, copper-colored, with broad, flat noses, and red hair, who are active and robust.

Previous to that some similar statements had been made. An accurate description of the people of the Val de Ribas (Province of Gerona) is to be found in 'Kosmos,' May, 1887. Macpherson found them, especially in the Collado de Tosas; and he lays stress on the fact that they have often been considered to be cretins, but that both cretins and dwarfs are found in that district. Their hair is described as being 'mahogany-colored wool.'

Unfortunately Mr. Haliburton from ill-health was prevented from confirming his conclusions as to them by personally enquiring on the spot as to these matters.

From the comments in the preceding paper, written by Herr von Lushan (on Mr. David MacRitchie's paper on 'Pygmies in Spain,' in the *International Archive for Ethnography*) it seems very desirable that a specialist well versed in such matters (cretinism and dwarfism in the Pyrenees) should carefully enquire into this subject on the spot.[3]

FOOTNOTES

[1] A very malformed dwarf, named "Wambutti," which was reported to be a Mogrebin, accompanied the group of Denka blacks exhibited in Berlin in 1889.

[[2] Until Ebers suggested that Pount was situated in the far East, Pount, Put, or Phut, was held to be connected with Libya, and, according to Bunsen, "is admitted to mean, in the strictest sense, Mauritania.". J. G. Müller, in his *Die Semiten*, says, "The old suggestion that Put refers to the Libyans is confirmed by Champollion, and also by Bunsen (I., 572)."—R. G. H.]

[[3] Mr. MacRitchie's visit only lasted two or three days, as it was cut short by the state of the weather and of the roads. For the same reason he was unable to visit the village of Aledo, on the summit of a mountain near the railway from Carthagena to Grenada, which is inhabited by "little people" and Gypsies. The dwarfs live in houses resembling "weems," and built of large stones covered with earth. Their industry, like that of some of the Atlas dwarfs, consists of making mats from Esparto grass. In 1892-3, Mr. Walter B. Harris, author of "Tafilet," and other books of travel, was urged by me to make enquiries at the Val de Ribas, and I offered to pay the expenses of such a visit; but he declined.—R.G.H.]

THE DWARF DOMESTIC ANIMALS OF PYGMIES

R. G. Haliburton

For years I have enjoyed the honor of being a corresponding member of the Institute, but up to the present I have contributed nothing to its Transactions. If I have not shared the fate of the proverbial "unproductive fig tree," it is due to the forbearance of the Institute, and their charitable hope that, if spared by them, I might do better in future.

It is, therefore, with great pleasure that I offer my first instalment, a paper of interest, not on account of the way its subject is dealt with, but because it opens up for the first time an untrodden field of science that is likely, in proper hands, to yield important results. Whatever will hereafter account for the diminutive size of the domestic animals of pygmies, will also explain the origin of the dwarf races of men; and, possibly, this may be true vice versa.

One of my most persistent critics was, among my friends, called "fascinating subject," as this was a pet term of his. Judge my dismay in June last, on reading in an article on "Pygmy Races," the following ominous sentence, with which it begins: "Professor Starr's article on 'Pygmy Races of Men' in *The North American Review* contains much interesting information regarding a curious and fascinating subject."

To my relief I found that he admitted most fully all my contentions. The existence of dwarf tribes in the Atlas, similar to the Akkas of Equatorial Africa, "had been demonstrated"; that there are diminutive Nanos in the Pyrenees was also admitted; and also that strong evidence had been adduced as to the existence of dwarf survivals in America. I could hardly believe that the writer was my old friend but for a significant omission. He fully accepted my discoveries, but forgot to mention my name in connection with them. Still, to have converted him to that extent was eminently satisfactory.

He concludes with some very sensible remarks, which are especially interesting in connection with an even still more fascinating subject, "The Dwarf Domestic Animals of Pygmies." "It is evident that the existence of pygmy races has passed out of the region of myth and fable into that of history and science. Our information regarding these strange races is still incomplete and inexact, but it is being steadily augmented and brought in line with accepted results in biology and anthropology. The facts already adduced suggest many interesting reflections, but, perhaps raise more problems than they solve. It seems clearly impossible (?) to regard the pygmy races as owning a common origin, although their tendency to conform to a single fairly well-defined type is very curious.

"Is their case one of degeneration, owing to some special circumstances of climate and environment, or do they represent a remnant still remaining in a stage of development long since left behind by the rest of the human species? We cannot say with certainty, but such questions may yet become capable of solution, when our information on the subject has become more extensive and exact."

In 1800, when I visited Morocco to look into the subject of racial dwarfs there, one of my first informants as to their small animals was a halfbreed dwarf at Tangier, about four feet high, who is to be seen in the Soko, or market place there. In my "Dwarfs of Mount Atlas" (p. 25), we find him say, "The dwarfs are very brave, and great hunters of ostriches, having small, swift horses, that are called by a name, meaning 'those that drink the wind,' and that are fed on dates and camels' milk, and are very lean, and, judged by their looks, would be set down as worthless. This description of these ostrich hunters agreed with that given me by my Berber servant in 1888." A rabbi from Ternata, on the Dra, also said (see p. 29), "There are many of them (the dwarfs) near the Soudan. The Arabs fear them, and pay to be allowed to pass through their country. Their horses can do without water for four days, and are called *dwiminagh* ('they that drink the wind')."

There is a place called Adwarfi, two or three days to the south-east of Tafilet, which is a great resort of the dwarfs, and a part of the Saharan Atlas is called the Black Mountains, where is the River Dora, and where there are many caves, in which the dwarfs live with their cattle. They have an Arabic name, meaning "the people that own cattle." A little Ait Atta from near Adwarfi, and also afterwards a Jew from that region, described the dwarfs there as living in hillocks, in which there are very small entrances, leading to a central chamber, into which, at night, they drive their cattle, which are very small. Mr. MacRitchie, in his "Testimony

of Tradition," speaks of the "weems" of Scotland, which are
precisely similar structures to the hillocks of the Sahara;
and in one of them, he says, in its central chamber were
found the bones of a small ox.

In 1893 Mr. Carlo Bruzeau, of the Villa de France Hotel
at Tangier, told me that twenty years ago, during a time of
famine, he "saw a man bringing into Mogador for sale a
string of shaggy ponies. When asked whence they came,
the Moor replied, 'From the mountains (the Saharan Atlas);
there, horses, sheep, goats, cows, men, all are very small.'"

In the same year the dwarf tribe that inhabits the Great
Atlas, not much more, than a day's journey from the City
of Morocco, were described to me as owning little sheep,
donkeys, goats and cows; and a Moor offered to bring some
to Mogador, should I wish to buy some of them.

The Barbary donkey is well known, a pretty, tiny specimen of the breed, generally black, and very active and
strong for its size.

Nearly always, wherever pygmy tribes exist, or must
have once existed, we find very small domestic animals.
Bent, in his "Mashonaland," says that they are very diminutive throughout South Africa. This even extends to the poultry. A hen's egg there is hardly larger than a pigeon's egg.

This is also the case in Europe. Wherever there are survivals or very distinct traditions of early dwarf races, there
we invariably find small breeds of domestic animals. In
Brittany we not only have occasional survivals of very small
people, but also very diminutive cows and ponies. In Shetland and the Hebrides we have very conclusive traditions
as to dwarfs, and there, too, we find little Shetland ponies,

small "black-faced sheep," etc. In Wales, too, with its under-sized, dark-complexioned people, we meet with little Welsh sheep and cows. In the same way in Kerry, where the tales of the Skillimilinks, and "the little red-headed blacks" are to be met with, there we have the same types of animals. The little Kerry cows are famed for their good qualities. In Galloway, too, in South-western Scotland, where history tells us of the warlike, small-sized Pechts, who claimed the right to lead the van in armies, we find the well-known ponies called "Galloways," as well as small cows.

The popular belief of the herdsmen and cheesemakers (Macaires) of the Vosges Mountains, not only that there are pygmy herdsmen there, who dwell in caves in the pre-cipitous cliffs of that region, but also that these dwarfs have dwarf cattle, is most interesting. On this point I may quote the following passages from my paper on "Dwarf Surviv-als and Traditions as to Pygmy Races."

"Thirteen years ago my attention was attracted by the name of some cliff dwellers in Abyssinia, which Jean Tem-poral, in his translation of an early Portuguese book on that country, calls 'Vosges.' As I had, in 1863, suggested (see Haliburton, 'New Materials for the History of Man' [1863], pp. 14, 23, and note, 41, 74) that there must have been a migration from Africa to Europe in early ages, I made a note of these facts, intending some day to enquire whether there are not traces of cliff dwellings, or cliff dwellers, in the mountainous country of Alsace, 'the Vosges.' In 1892, as Admiral Blomfield Pasha, of Alexandria, and Mrs. Blomfield, were about to spend six weeks in the Vosges, I asked them to look into the question. In a few weeks I received a local guide-book, which more than bore out my anticipations. In the *Guide Joanne*, Geradmer (Paris, Libr. Hachette & Cie, p. 26), we are told that La Schaume, of Nisheim, which surrounds Wurtzelstein, it is believed, is inhabited by a kindly-disposed race of dwarfs, who, when the herdsmen descend to the lower valleys with their herds in the autumn, pasture their cattle, which are of very small size, in the upper pastures, and make cheese till the spring. Among different authorities cited is 'The Foyer Alsacien,' by Chas. Grad." "In 1893 (*i.e.*, after I had heard from Blomfield Pasha), I learned in Morocco that, two days south of the Great Atlas, there is a high mountain called Voshe, the inhabitants of which are dwarf cave-dwellers who are called Ait Voshe (the Voshe Tribe). Professor Schlichter says that the Akka dwarfs of Equatorial Africa are known to their neighbors as Voshu, and also Tiki-Tiki, names connected with the Akka dwarfs of southern Morocco, who are also called Jed-ibwa 'the Father of our Fathers.'"

The range of the name for dwarfs, Tiki, or Tiki-Tiki, is almost world-wide.[1] When the Akka, or Tiki-Tiki of Equatorial Africa wandered north to Europe, they must have brought their diminutive cattle with them, for in Baker's "Albert Nyanza" (1866, p. 91), a region where the wide-spread Akka, or Voshu, are to be found, we are told that "the cattle there are very small. The goats and sheep are quite Liliputian."

In Ceylon, the original inhabitants of which are the little Veddahs (called often "Devil-dancers"), there is a very diminutive breed of sacred oxen, whose small size is put down to some wonderful myth about Buddha. These oxen are very nimble-footed, and are used in carriages by the natives, as they can easily travel eight miles an hour. A friend of mine told me recently that in a part of Bengal where he lives, there is a similar breed of oxen, and that it is considered by the rich Hindoos the correct thing to have a carriage drawn by six or eight of them.

But all this was known to the ancients over 2,000 years ago. Ctesias, a physician of Artaxerxes, who travelled in Asia, and described the pygmy race that he there saw, says that they owned diminutive flocks, sheep the size of a lamb, small donkeys and oxen, and horses and mules not larger than a ram is in Greece. (See *Ctesiae fragmenta*, No. 57, II, Didot).

Aristotle states that the Pygmies live near the lakes from which the Nile flows, "and this is no fable, for there is really, it is said, a race of dwarfs, both men and horses, which lead the life of Troglodytes." (See *Hist. Animal*, VIII. 2).

Strabo, who was a sceptic as to the pygmies, though he described small races of men, says of the Western Ethiopians (evidently the dwarfs of the Dra and the northern Sahara, whom I have alluded to), "their mode of life is wretched. They are, for the most part, naked, and wander from place to place with their flocks. Their flocks and herds are small in size, whether sheep, goats or oxen; the dogs also, though fierce and quarrelsome, are small." (See Bohn's *Classical Library*, Vol. III., p. 270, 1857.)

It was pointed out in 1891, in my "Dwarfs of Mount Atlas," that pygmies are supposed in northern Morocco and in Nubia to be Cyclops, and that, as the dwarfs of the Atlas, like other natives of southern Morocco, wear a singular bournous, on the back of which is worked an immense eye, a yard in length, "the people with the eye" must in time have become "the people with only one eye." This view, as well as my contention that the dwarfs of the Atlas have little domestic animals, are confirmed by Robert Brown, Jr., who in his "Neptune," says that the Cyclops of the Odyssey were an agricultural people of North Africa, who had diminutive cattle, the milk of which yielded very rich cream.

I have omitted to refer to two curious points: that there are in several isolated and inaccessible localities in the Southern States little communities composed of survivals of those pygmy tribes that have disappeared from the west coast of Africa; and also that there are on the Atlantic seaboard little ponies, the descendants, probably, of a small breed that belonged to these dwarfs, and that were shipped with them to America. Strange to say, their name is "Teki horses."

Dr. Weir's interesting article in *The Popular Science Monthly* for June, 1896, on "The Pygmy in the United States" (which, however, does not refer to these small horses), will well repay a perusal.

I invite the attention, not only of anthropologists, but also of zoologists, to this subject: Are these little breeds the original stock, and have domestic animals gradually become larger and stronger, just as cultivated plants have; or have scores of thousands of years of privation dwarfed them and their pygmy owners?

It is very desirable that zoologists should carefully study and apply the investigations of Yale naturalists and palaeontologists as to the origin of the horse in America, which would seem to indicate that the ordinary horse had an even smaller prototype than the little "drinkers of the wind" of the Sahara, in a fox-like animal with five toes, developing in later ages into a larger, horse-like animal with a cloven foot. "After that the deluge"—some catastrophe that put a final stop to horse-raising in America in primordial times.

I also suggest a point which zoologists may follow up with good results.

Mr. Cunninghame Graham, three or four years ago, in an article on Argentina, said that the horse of the Pampas differs from the ordinary horse, the lumbar vertebrae of which are one more in number than those of the Pampas horses. This, he said, also applies to Barbs, and he thought that the Spaniards must have brought out Moorish horses with them to Argentina. I tried, when last in Morocco, to get a skeleton of a Barbary horse examined by a veterinary surgeon, but did not succeed. If the Barb differs also from ordinary horses, it probably got its peculiarity from the little breed of ponies in the Sahara. It is very important to ascertain whether the latest type of fossil horses in America resembled the Barbs or the common horse in this respect.[2]

Henceforth we have immensely improved chances of solving the problems of the origins of small breeds of domestic animals, and of pygmy races of men—for what will explain the one, will also settle the other.

As respects the latter, the tendency of scientific thought is to regard dwarf races of men as having been the original and earliest specimens of humanity on the earth, and to yield to them the place so long occupied by a supposed "missing link." The latest traveller in Africa, Professor Donaldson Smith, writing last summer to *The World* an account of Abyssinian dwarfs discovered by him, says: "Although they live among other native tribes, they differ totally from them as respects their principal ethnological features. This fact strengthens the theory that the African pygmies are not degenerate specimens of the tribes among whom they live, but are the remnants of the first and original population of the Dark Continent."

Mgr. Lerey, Papal Nuncio to East Africa, says the same thing, and asserts that the dwarfs think so, too, and despise all the larger races as *parvenus*. They claim to be the first, and oldest, and noblest inhabitants of Africa.

It may be worthy of mention that a review of the latest book on Anthropology, Hutchinson's "Prehistoric Man and Beast" (Appletons, N.Y.), says: "Certain analogies lend weight to the idea that possibly Stonehenge was erected by the dwarfs or fairies, who, in a previous chapter, are shown to have been a real people. Various writers have come to the conclusion that a dwarf population akin to the Laps were the actual inhabitants of the 'fairy knowes,' or underground megalithic structures, and became in time the elves and fairies of folk-lore."

The following is an extract from a letter received from Professor Putnam, President of the American Association for the Advancement of Science, dated September 3, 1897:

"I have not forgotten my promise to send you a memorandum about the horse's tooth found at the ruins of Copan. I send you by this mail, addressed the same as this letter, a copy of the *Memoir* giving the report of the museum explorations in Copan. On page 31 you will find a mention of the horse's tooth which was discovered in an ancient tomb in the ruins of Copan. Mr. Saville, who excavated the tomb, does not see any possibility of the tooth having got into the tomb after it was made; and it seems hardly probable, although some burrowing animal might have carried it into the tomb. This tooth is either that of the well-known post-pliocene horse of America, the *Equus fraternus* of Leidy, or it is the tooth of the introduced *E. caballus* of Europe. It is impossible from the tooth alone to determine which animal it belongs to. The similarity is so close that Dr. Wortman, who is the best authority on this subject, is not willing to risk his reputation by saying to which species this tooth belongs.

"Of course, if there is no doubt about this tooth having been buried in pre-Columbian times, it settles the question of the co-existence of the horse with the early inhabitants of Copan, unless they obtained a fossil tooth belonging to the post-pliocene period and put it in this tomb.

"Some authors are of the opinion that the horse was in existence on this continent at the time of the advent of the Europeans. You will find a statement made by Sebastian Cabot after his expedition to the Rio la Plata in 1527, where he says he saw horses at a distance. The fact that the remains of horses have been found in post-pliocene deposits in the southern portions of America certainly makes it possible that the horse may have co-existed with early man in that region. Still, if this is the case, it is very strange that we have not found the remains of the horse abundant in

prehistoric sites, and that we do not find the horse represented in the sculpture and drawings of any of our early
peoples. Again, if the horse was in existence in America, it
hardly seems possible that the Mexicans would have been
so wonder-struck by the appearance of Cortes and his men
mounted on horses.

"So you see the question is regarded as an open one. I
hope you may settle it."

[The above letter suggests the query: May not the horse
have existed in pre-Columbian times without having been
utilized as a beast of burthen or for the saddle? Whence
did the breed of Indian ponies come? R. G. H.]

FOOTNOTES

[1] See "The Tiki-Tiki," page 88.

[2] After this paper was written it was found that the fossil horse
resembled the Barb in this respect. The following paragraph appeared
in *The New York Evening Post*, July 10th, 1897: "A curiosity recently
seen at the Salt Lake stock yards was an 'Aztec' horse, 36 inches
high, and weighing 290 lbs. It was caught in Arizona." Can it be possible that the American horse has left a pony representative? The odds
against its existence are very great. The probability is that the little
horse is the descendant of a "teki" pony that had been brought west
by some immigrant. The point, however, is worth enquiry.

COMMENTS

Professor Frederick Starr

When De Quatrefages wrote his work in 1887, a presentation of the views of the ancients and a study of African *nigrillos* and Asiatic *negritos* was exhaustive of the subject of the pygmies. But now the question presents other phases. In 1888 and 1891, in papers by Mr. R. G. Haliburton, the existence of a race of dwarfs in the Atlas Mountains of southern Morocco was announced. A strangely acrimonious and personal discussion followed, which was prolonged through a number of years. It seems that now we must add a fifth—a Northern or Moroccan group to the four groups of African pygmies already known. Mr. Haliburton, prevented by ill-health from journeying to these pygmies, lost no opportunity of securing information. From sixty-five different persons he has secured a considerable mass of evidence. Villages or tribes of these Atlas dwarfs have been located in the districts of Akka and Sus, in the Dra Valley, in places to the south-east of Dra and at other points. A number of different names are applied to them—the Little Harateen, Akkas, Nezeegan, etc. They are reported to be about four feet high, with a reddish ("mahogany") complexion and short woolly hair. They are active and brave.

They often perform as acrobats, are 'good at singlestick,' and are 'skilled in hunting ostriches, the feathers and eggs of which they sell to Arab traders of the Sahara. They are not diligent at manual labor, but know cobbling, tinkering, etc. They are reported to use in ostrich hunting small, swift horses that are called 'those that drink the wind.' These are fed on dates and camels' milk, and are lean and look worthless. These pygmies are said to use poisoned arrows. When at home they wear a woollen shirt embroidered at the front and back; red leather leggings that nearly come to the knee, and a knife with a curious crescent-shaped handle. They live on milk and camel-flesh; the meat is pounded, salted, and packed away in goatskins. A handful of this will suffice for a man's subsistence two days. Authorities differ in regard to the religious belief of these dwarfs; quite possibly the populations really differ among themselves. Some are reputed to worship Didoo Osiri; most of them are considered Christians or half-Christians, 'as they shave their faces and the front of their heads.' ... The big neighbors of all these little people look upon them with curiously mingled feelings of reverence, dislike, and fear. 'They bring good luck and are not to be talked about.' They largely get their living by writing charms and telling fortunes; 'they know the stars well'; and find money for people by writing on wooden slates. Such are the dwarfs of the Atlas. Is it not likely that their ancestors—and not those of the Akkas of Central Africa—are the dwarf Troglodytes, who, according to Herodotus, captured the five young Nasamonians? On an Egyptian monument, perhaps four thousand years old, is a quaint picture of a dwarf with the word 'Akka';

before that picture was painted, perhaps a thousand years before, an inscription (discussed by Professor Sayce) tells of a Denga dwarf 'who danced divinely' like one that had been brought still earlier to King Assa of the fifth dynasty. These three dwarfs of Egyptian picture and inscription probably came from this Atlas region, perhaps from the very district called Akka to-day. The recurrence of this name Akka in two widely separated regions in connection with dwarf peoples is interesting, and suggests ancient relationship between Schweinfurth's Central African and Haliburton's Moroccan dwarfs.

The question of dwarf races in Europe is now under discussion. The Roman anthropologist, Sergi, has found small skulls and skeletons in the old *Kungaas* of Russia, from the Chersonese to Novoladoga, and from Kasan and Astrakhan to Minsk. Remains of this same pygmy race have been found by him in ancient graves in Sicily, Sardinia, and about Naples. This population was certainly shorter than the Mincopies of the Andamans, and was more like the *nigrillos* than the *negritos*. Still more, both in Russia and in Italy he finds evidence of this pygmy folk in the living population. In this connection he emphasizes the fact that in certain districts of Italy from thirteen per cent. to sixteen per cent, of the persons examined by the recruiting officers fall below the required stature. He describes this European pygmy race as from 1.25 metres to 1.5 metres in height, with a brain capacity from 300 to 400 cubic centimetres less than the Italian average. Sergi suggests a theory in regard to this Italian and Russian population. He believes in an early migration of pygmies from Africa northward into the Mediterranean islands, Italy and eastern Europe. In May, 1894, Dr. Kollman, of Basel, Switzerland, called attention to little skeletons and skulls found at Schweizerbild, near Schaffhausen. The skeletons were apparently of Neolithic Age. Two kinds were found, some of ordinary sized individuals presenting the types still represented in Europe; others were of little people, averaging perhaps 1.424 metres in stature. Out of thirteen skeletons of adults found, four were small. Kollman believes these were the same as Sergi found further south.

Some years ago a Prof. Morayta wrote a paper concerning the Nanos of the Pyrenees. The paper attracted no attention, and perhaps was never printed in full. Mr. Haliburton learned of it, and has looked into the matter.

Morayta's description of Nanos is at times, almost word for word, the same as the description of cretins, as given by Baillarger and Krishaber in the *Dictionnaire Encyclopedique des Sciences Medicales.* It is not then strange that many have believed the Pyrenean dwarfs to be not a pygmy race, but cretins. It was necessary that some competent person should look into the question on the spot. Accordingly, in May, 1894, Mr. David MacRitchie visited the region to look for Nanos. Bad weather compelled a short trip, but in four days he found eleven cases. Some of these were plainly cretinous. In concluding his article *(Archiv. für Ethnographie,* Vol. VIII.), he says: 'I am inclined to regard them as the remnants of a race. Undoubtedly cretinism and goitre enter into the question. But of the eleven dwarfs whom I saw in the Ribas neighborhood, only two were affected with goitre. It is hard to believe that the little woman who figures first on my list owes her small stature and her other characteristics to the working of disease. And if those peculiarities are simply the outward signs of cretinism, and if cretinism is due to environment, how comes it that other people, living exactly the same life, are absolutely free from any such defects of mind or body?' Mr. Haliburton calls the cretin theory 'hasty.' He says: 'The Denga dwarfs are the same now as five thousand years ago. We do not hear of goitre' (which is curiously related to cretinism; the children of goitrous parents are likely to be cretins; cretinism is never found in regions or among populations where goitre does not exist) 'among the robust and warlike pygmies of the Great Lakes and Congo, who are flesheaters and hunters. I am persuaded that if a child of a Pyrenean cretin were to be fed on flesh food and made to lead an active life, he would never show any trace of goitre on arriving at manhood.' The paragraph shows a lack of clear knowledge regarding goitre and cretinism, but the line of argument is clear. He also says: 'Neither cretinism nor any other disease can turn ordinary Europeans into pygmies, with broad, flat noses, a copper-colored complexion, and mahogany-colored wool.' ... 'Cretinism does not attack their larger neighbors, who for many centuries have lived near them. Cretinism in the Pyrenees and Alps, it seems to me, is racial in its character, and is not a disease, but a symptom of decadence in a moribund race of dwarfs, who in the recesses of mountains are slowly going through the process of dying out through failing vitality, just as many centuries ago their race must have died out on the plains of Europe and Asia.' ... 'The question of the Pyrenean dwarfs is a delicate one.

We need much further study before they can be admitted
into the list of true pygmies. Just now Mr. Haliburton has
secured hints of dwarf peoples in the Black Forest, the
Vosges, and in Frisian districts. In this article we do not
pretend to go outside the somatological field, otherwise we
should present the very interesting matter drawn by Mr.
MacRitchie and Mr. Haliburton, from linguistics, legend
and folk-lore, relative to European pygmies or "little
people."'

At the last two meetings of the American Association for
the Advancement of Science, Mr. Haliburton has brought
up the question of pygmy peoples in America. Hints of such
are not wanting. Some things about the ruined buildings of
Yucatan and Central America suggest that they were built
by little people. At Uxmal there is a 'house of the dwarf,'
and at Cozumel are little buildings. In 1887 Brigham wrote
in his 'Guatemala': 'It would certainly be interesting to
learn why many of the temples have doors, passages, and
even rooms, that a man of ordinary stature cannot stand
erect in.' The Peabody Museum explorations in Central
America have brought to light a number of representations
of dwarfs. Haliburton describes one of these as having 'a
square, broad, and flat face; Mongolian eyes; bulging
cheeks, more prominent than the broad and flat nose.' Various writers have commented upon little Mexicans. In 1882
a band of little people invaded British Honduras. They were
from four feet to four feet six inches in stature, and are
said to be warlike, to make human sacrifices, to use the
blow-gun and poisoned arrows, and to be makers of Panama
hats. Mrs. Le Plongeon mentions a dwarf woman captured

in Yucatan. Dwarf tribes are said to live, or to have lived, in Brazil, Uruguay, and other parts of South America.

At Mr. Haliburton's suggestion our party last summer looked in Mexico for evidence of pygmy peoples there. No very definite information was secured. At Aguas Calientes, with a population of perhaps 30,000, we saw seven adults, none more than four feet eight inches in stature, in a single half hour. An Indian at Lake Chapala declared that there were little people in the mountains somewhere in Jalisco or Colima. Near Aytzcapatzalco, a suburb of the City of Mexico, are some full-blooded Indians who retain their old dress and are very conservative, and of little stature; they are probably Otomis. Little people live near Cholula. All of these hints may lead to something when followed up. Meantime the question whether there are pygmy tribes in America seems to be really propounded.

Obituary:
Robert Grant Haliburton

Stansbury Hagar

Robert Grant Haliburton.—Robert Grant Haliburton, M.A., Q.C., D.C.L., was born at Windsor, Nova Scotia, June 3, 1831, and died at Pass Christian, Miss., March 14, 1901. He was the elder son of the Honorable Thomas Chandler Haliburton, the well-known jurist, writer, and member of Parliament, whose "Sam Slick" papers justly earned him the title of "father of American humor."

Following in the footsteps of his father, the son graduated from King's College, Windsor, with high honors. Within a year thereafter he was called to the provincial bar, where his exceptional ability soon became apparent. Removing to Ottawa shortly after, he established there an extensive practice. Amongst his most important legal successes were the settlement of the Prince Edward Island land disputes in 1860, and the determination of the legal status of fugitive slaves in Canada.

Owing to the belief shared by father and son that the publication of one of the former's works had prejudiced a certain section of the electorate against both, Mr. Haliburton declined to accept office under the Canadian government, but he was nevertheless able to make himself a factor of

232

importance in politics as well as in the organization of various commercial associations.

A passage in Rivero and Tschudi's antiquities of Peru led Mr. Haliburton to take up the study of the astronomical element in primitive myths and ceremonials. The result of his studies as revealed in his *New Material for the History of Mankind*—unfortunately a very rare work—proved the existence of a world-wide cult founded on the worship of the Pleiades as the stars of rain and the harvest. This cult was shown to have arisen from the use of the Pleiades as time markers, their position being such as to afford the simplest, and therefore the earliest discovered, means of defining seed time and harvest. Mr. Haliburton's researches in this field have been extensively used by other well-known writers, such as F. Piazzi Smith in his *Life and Work at the Great Pyramid*, Blake in his *Astronomical Myths*, and Bunsen in his *Der Plejarden und der Thierkriess*, the last-named work being dedicated to him. He may reasonably be regarded as the pioneer of modern science in the field of symbolical astronomy.

In 1881, while at Tangier, he began the collection of notes on the folklore and mythology of Morocco. This led to the discovery of the existence of racial dwarfs in and near the Atlas mountains and won for the discoverer the medal of the Ninth Oriental Congress. In spite of this recognition, however, "Mr. Haliburton's dwarfs" as they were termed, were regarded with incredulity by many, some writers assuming a tone which seemed to somewhat pass the bounds of legitimate criticism. But these critics were soon discomforted by the acceptance of the "little people" as true racial dwarfs by such authorities as Virchow and Sayce. This discovery induced Mr. Haliburton to suspect the possible existence of dwarfs elsewhere, in spite of the prevailing ignorance on the subject. Traces of them were found in the Pyrenees and other parts of Europe, and more conclusive evidence in Central America, Peru, and the Amazon country. Various indications seemed to suggest that the dwarfs might once have been a widely distributed race, possibly synonymous with pre-glacial man; but Mr. Haliburton realized that the available evidence is not yet sufficient to establish such a theory, therefore he wisely abstained from presenting it. In 1897 he privately published at Toronto his various papers on the dwarfs in a volume entitled, *How a Race of Pygmies were Found in North Africa and Spain.*

Personally all those who have met him will remember him as a most genial and kindly man, who took an earnest and unselfish interest in all scientific research. Honest, fearless, yet cautious, with eyes wide open to see, tolerant of all views in the belief that even error, if honest, points the way to truth, and always courteous, even to those critics who passed the bounds of courtesy, it was not alone by his researches that science has profited, for his influence over others was as important as his work. To it we owe the Micmac studies of the late Dr. S. T. Rand, besides several well-known works in the region where astronomy and anthropology meet. Nor was that influence confined to the scientific field. Perhaps the best known of Canadian poets, now deceased, declared that he and his companions had learned to look upon Mr. Haliburton as a father who was ever ready with suggestion and encouragement. Such was the man whose loss all must deplore.

Sources

A number of Haliburton's papers were collected in his self-published anthology, *How a Race of Pygmies Was Found in North Africa and Spain* (1897, Toronto). Some other sources included:

NOTES ON MOUNT ATLAS AND ITS TRADITIONS
Proceedings of the American Association for the Advancement of Science,
 Vol. XXXI., Montreal Meeting, August, 1882.

RACIAL DWARFS IN THE ATLAS AND THE PYRENEES
The Imperial and Asiatic Quarterly Review and Oriental and Colonial Record,
 Vol. VI (Nos. 11-12); 1893.

SURVIVALS OF DWARF RACES IN THE NEW WORLD
Proceedings of the American Association for the Advancement of Science,
 Vol. XLIII, 1894.

DWARF SURVIVALS, AND TRADITIONS AS TO PYGMY RACES
Proceedings of the American Association for the Advancement of Science, Vol.
 XLIV, 1895.

OBITUARY
American Anthropologist, Vol. 3 (No. 2), 1901

ANCIENT
AND
MEDIEVAL DYES

William F. Leggett

ANCIENT AND MEDIEVAL DYES
Available from Coachwhip Publications

COACHWHIP PUBLICATIONS

CoachwhipBooks.com

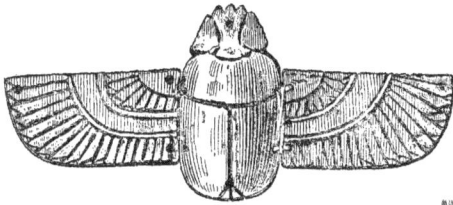

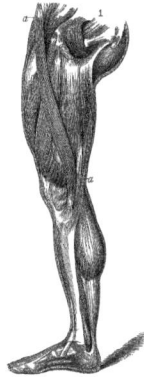

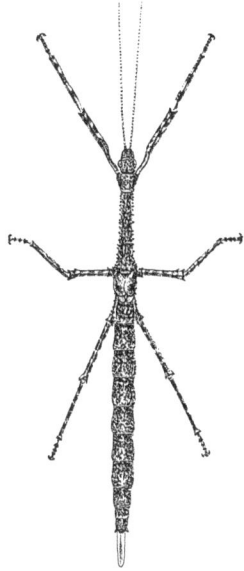

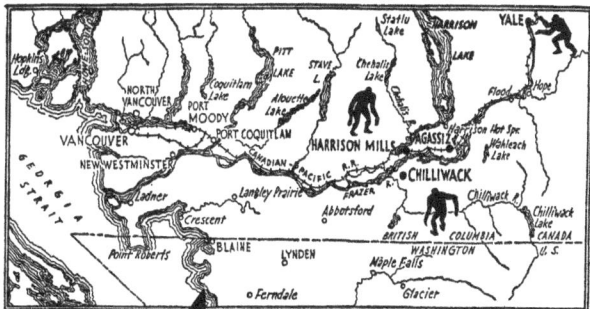

www.ingramcontent.com/pod-product-compliance
Lightning Source LLC
Chambersburg PA
CBHW030006290326
41934CB00005B/248